KABBALAH

A STUDY OF THE

TEN LUMINOUS
EMANATIONS

TALMUD   ESSER   SFIROT

KABBALAH

A STUDY OF THE
TEN LUMINOUS
EMANATIONS

VOLUME ONE

THE WISDOM OF THE KABBALAH BY
RABBI YEHUDA ASHLAG z"l

AS REVEALED BY THE WRITINGS OF
RABBI ISAAC LURIA z"l

COMPILED AND EDITED BY

RABBI PHILIP S. BERG

FIRST EDITION
January 1994

ISBN 0-924457-91-0 (Soft cover)

For further information:

RESEARCH CENTRE OF KABBALAH
85-03 114th Street, Richmond Hill
NEW YORK, 11418

— or —

P.O. BOX 14168
THE OLD CITY, JERUSALEM

NEW YORK (718) 805-9122
LOS ANGELES (310) 657-5404
MEXICO CITY (525) 589-4464
TORONTO (416) 631-9395
PARIS (331) -43-56-01-38
TEL AVIV (03) 528-0570
BUENOS AIRES (541)-381-0025

PRINTED IN U.S.A.

It is with a joyful heart
that I sponsor this book
in honor of my parents
my guiding force

Dave Salvit z"l
A gentle, wise and caring father

and

Mina Salvit
A loving, patient mother

For my wife

KAREN

*In the vastness of cosmic space
and the infinity of lifetimes,
it is my bliss to share
a soulmate and
an age of Aquarius
with you.*

ABOUT THE CENTRES

Kabbalah is mystical Judaism. It is the deepest and most hidden meaning of the Torah, or Bible. Through the ultimate knowledge and mystical practices of Kabbalah, one can reach the highest spiritual levels attainable. Although many people rely on belief, faith, and dogmas in pursuing the meaning of life, the unknown, and the unseen, Kabbalists seek a spiritual connection with the Creator and the forces of the Creator, so that the strange becomes familiar, and faith becomes knowledge.

Throughout history, those who knew and practiced the Kabbalah were extremely careful in their dissemination of the knowledge — for they knew the masses of mankind had not yet prepared for the ultimate truth of existence. Today Kabbalists know, through Kabbalistic knowledge, that it is not only proper but necessary to make available the Kabbalah to all who seek it.

The Research Centre of Kabbalah is an independent, non-profit institute founded in Israel in 1922. The Centre provides research, information, and assistance to those who seek the insights of Kabbalah. The Centre offers public lectures, classes, seminars, and excursions to mystical sites at branches in Israel — in Jerusalem, Tel Aviv, Haifa, Beer Sheva, Ashdod, and Ashkelon— and in the United States in New York and Los Angeles. Branches have been opened in Mexico, Montreal, Toronto, Paris, Hong Kong and Taiwan. Thousands of people have benefited by the Centre's activities, and the Centre's publishing of Kabbalistic material continues to be the most comprehensive of its kind in the world including translations in English, Hebrew, Russian, German, Portuguese, French, Spanish, Farsi (Persian) and Chinese.

Kabbalah can provide one with the true meaning of their being and the knowledge necessary for their ultimate benefit. It can show one spirituality which is beyond belief. The Research Centre of Kabbalah will continue to make available the Kabbalah to all those who seek it.

ABOUT THE ZOHAR

The ZOHAR, the basic source of the Kabbalah was written by Rabbi Shimon bar Yohai while hiding from the Romans in a cave in Pe'quin for 13 years. It was later brought to light by Rabbi Moses de Leon in Spain and further revealed through the Safed Kabbalists and the Lurianic system of Kabbalah.

The programs of the Research Centre of Kabbalah have been established to provide opportunities for learning, teaching, research, and demonstration of specialized knowledge drawn from the ageless wisdom of the Zohar and the Jewish sages. Long kept from the masses, today this knowledge should be shared by all who seek to understand the deeper meaning of our Jewish heritage, a more profound meaning of life. Modern science is only beginning to discover what our sages veiled in symbolism. This knowledge is of a very practical nature and can be applied daily for the betterment of our lives and of humankind.

Our courses and materials deal with the Zoharic understanding of each weekly portion of the Torah. Every facet of Jewish life is covered and other dimensions, hitherto unknown, provide a deeper connection to a superior Reality. Three important beginning courses cover such aspects as: Time, Space and Motion; Reincarnation, Marriage, Divorce, Kabbalistic Meditation, Limitation of the five senses, Illusion-Reality, Four Phases, Male and Female, Death, Sleep, Dreams; Food: what is kosher and why; Circumcision, Redemption of the First Born, Shatnes, Shabbat.

Darkness cannot prevail in the presence of Light. A darkened room must respond even to the lighting of a candle. As we share this moment together we are beginning to witness, and indeed some of us are already participating in a people's revolution of enlightenment. The darkened clouds of strife and conflict will make their presence felt only as long as the Eternal Light remains concealed.

The Zohar now remains a final, if not the only, solution to infusing the cosmos with the revealed Light of the Force. The Zohar is not a book about religion. Rather, the Zohar is concerned with the relationship between the unseen forces of the cosmos, the Force, and the impact on Man.

The Zohar promises that with the ushering in of the Age of Aquarius the cosmos will become readily accessible to human understanding. It states that in the days of the Messiah "there will no longer be the necessity for one to request of his neighbor, teach me wisdom" (Zohar III, p.58a). "One day they will no longer teach every man his neighbor and every man his brother, saying know the Lord. For they shall all know Me, from the youngest to the oldest of them" (Jeremiah 31:34).

We can and must regain control of our lives and environment. To achieve this objective the Zohar provides us with an opportunity to transcend the crushing weight of universal negativity.

The daily perusing of the Zohar, without any attempt at translation or "understanding" will fill our consciousness with the Light, improving our well-being and influencing all in our environment toward positive attitudes. Even the scanning of the Zohar by those unfamiliar with the Hebrew Aleph Beth will accomplish the same result.

The connection that we establish through scanning the Zohar is a connection and unity with the Light of the Lord. The letters, even if we do not consciously know Hebrew or Aramaic, are the channels through which the connection is made and could be likened to dialing the right telephone number, or typing in the right codes to run a computer program. The connection is established at the metaphysical level of our being and radiates into our physical plane of existence...but first there is the metaphysical "fixing". We have to consciously, through positive thoughts and actions, permit the immense power of the Zohar to radiate love, harmony and peace into our lives for us to share with all humanity and the universe.

As we enter the years ahead, the Zohar will continue to be a people's book, striking a sympathetic chord in the hearts and minds of those who long for peace, truth and relief from suffering. In the face of crises and catastrophe it has the ability to resolve agonizing human afflictions by restoring each individual's relationship with the Force.

ABOUT THE EDITOR

RABBI PHILIP S. BERG is Dean of the Research Centre of Kabbalah. Born in New York City, into a family descended from a long line of Rabbis, he is an ordained Orthodox Rabbi (from the renowned rabbinical seminary Torat VaDaat). While traveling to Israel in 1962, he met his Kabbalistic master, Rabbi Yehuda Zvi Brandwein, student of Rabbi Yehuda Ashlag Z"L and then Dean of the Research Centre of Kabbalah. During that period the Centre expanded substantially with the establishment of the United States branch in 1965 through which it currently disseminates and distributes its publications. Rabbi Berg did research at the Centre under the auspices of his beloved teacher Rabbi Brandwein Z"L, writing books on such topics as the origins of Kabbalah, creation, cosmic consciousness, energy, and the myths of the speed of light and the light barrier. Following the death of his master in 1969, Rabbi Berg assumed the position of Dean of the Centre, expanding its publication program through the translation of source material on the Kabbalah into English and other languages. Rabbi Berg moved with his devoted and dedicated wife Karen to Israel in 1971, where they opened the doors of the Centre to all seekers of self identity, establishing centres in all major cities throughout Israel, while at the same time lecturing at the City University of Tel Aviv. They returned to the United States in 1981 to further establish centres of learning in major cities all over the world. In addition to publishing scientific and popular articles, Rabbi Berg is the author, translator and/or editor of eighteen other books, including the *Kabbalah for the Layman* series, *Wheels of a Soul, Time Zones, To the Power of One* and *Miracles, Mysteries, and Prayer* (two volumes).

ACKNOWLEDGEMENTS

I would like to express my gratitude to Roy Tarlow for reviewing the manuscript. He made fundamental contributions to the overall style. Many heartfelt thanks to him for his helpful suggestions and careful proofreading of the manuscript.

TABLE OF CONTENTS

VOLUME ONE

THE TREE OF LIFE
RESTRICTION[1] AND LINE OF LIGHT

[1] The terms "contraction" and "restriction" are used interchangeably in the following chapters.

FOREWORD

THE PRESENT SPIRITUAL REVIVAL IS phenomenal. but, unfortunately, with it have not come the answers to the demanding questions that have been raised. An endless amount of print has been devoted to the perplexing questions that man has been asking of himself, but to no avail. My intent is to demonstrate how the Kabbalah can solve man's perplexities.

What we can attempt through study of the Kabbalah is to understand the principle of cause and effect, that behind every effect lies a motivating cause. And in attempting this the Kabbalah makes various assumptions which, if within the entire universe we find no contradictions, then we must assume that these assumptions are correct.

The inability at times to understand the unseen cause is not detrimental to the process of evaluating a given situation, nor need this give us concern about not understanding the unseen cause. For example, in a theater one thousand people are told to observe a bottle on a table and then told to leave. After the theater has been totally emptied, all entrances are sealed from the outside. Several moments later the audience re-enters the theater, only to notice that the bottle is now resting on a chandelier. Everyone is certain that nobody has entered to remove the bottle from the table, yet obviously the bottle did not reach its destination by itself. The bottle is in the phase of effect, not cause, since a bottle cannot motivate or cause anything. Therefore, we can make the assumption that someone caused the bottle to be moved, although the cause has neither been determined nor seen.

As another example, the cause of, or reason for, narcotic addiction is often held to be poverty. How is this conclusion arrived at? Merely by observing a given situation or effect. For in the absence of a better reason, we latch on to what appears to be a justifiable cause so as to satisfy a substantial number of the effects. What we have conclusively failed to consider, however, is whether this cause satisfies each and every situation relating to narcotic addiction — which it doesn't. With further inquiry, it becomes apparent that poverty is not the true cause or reason, for narcotic addiction has also existed among the affluent. Thus, we must look again for the true cause.

True cause must be able to withstand tomorrow's events. For who can be so bold as to make predictions when one has not tasted or experienced the events of the future? One must be wary of those who advance their theories of tomorrow based only on present conditions limited by the narrow platform of time, space and motion; for the future, with its inevitable contradictions will disprove all the limited theories. Still, in the absence of any other method of forecasting future developments, our economists, scientists and ecologists must use this limited form of reasoning to provide an answer to the questions of present and future events. Also, we must recognize that the word "cause" is being misused, since cause is the direct motivating force behind every effect. And if we mistake the true nature of cause, we will not have faced the future effects and events with reality.

Our scientists glow with their technological advancements. And rightfully so, for a great deal of labor, time and money has gone into producing these advancements, which we shall assume have enhanced our lives. Yet (and in no way is the following statement meant to demean these advances), all that the scientist has done is merely discover something that already exists; that is, he has observed a reaction, but without knowing the true cause of this reaction. We may therefore conclude that, to some extent, the troubled times we are experiencing today can be directly related to the see-sawing events of cause and effect. Yet the cause advanced yesterday will not hold up tomorrow. This inevitably must create confusion and we find ourselves caught up in a variety of theories which, however, are not the true answers. Thus, despite scientific advances, the examination of the effects fails to disclose the hidden cause.

Our previous illustration of narcotic addiction (chosen because of its serious implication and effects on society) is classic. Two answers are advanced as to why the use of drugs is widespread; their availability and today's troubled times. These two causes, however, only give an insight into our convenient, symptomatic reasoning. For drugs have been known to mankind since time immemorial, and have always been available to the young and old alike. And needless to say we have had troubled times since the recording of history. Yet so-called qualified thinkers of our day will advance such apparently immature reasoning, believing that these are the causes. A true cause will have to avoid direct contradiction for it to be truly classified as the "cause". There is a cause, but it will have to withstand some very severe testing and constant questioning, paying heed to the limiting factors of time, space and motion.

Still another example, is the discovery by a medical, researcher that penicillin destroys streptococcus, yet without knowing why. The fact is that only through his observation is he certain that penicillin works. He only observes the effect; that is, the blackened area where the streptococcus is being destroyed. This is the extent of his discovery but he still lacks the true cause.

From the preceding we can conclude that (1) at times we accept a cause although it is unseen, and (2) even where it is quite apparent that the given cause will not hold up in every instance, still, if in the majority of cases it is plausible, it is acceptable. The Kabbalah offers a definite insight as to the true cause, which inevitably leads to the truth of cause and effect. From the causal precepts of the Kabbalah we discover a definite pattern, thereby convincing us of an omniscient Creator.

Let us now outline some of the questions Man has been asking of himself:

1. What is our existence all about?

2. What is our purpose in this endless chain of creation where we appear to be the least important, as compared to the wondrous worlds of the universe?

3. Self-reflection reveals our imperfections. Yet, how is this possible, seeing that we have been created by the Holy One, Whose perfect agency must necessarily produce perfect works?

4. One of the accepted assumptions of religious belief is that the Creator is All Good; therefore His intention must be to do all that is good. Why, then, did He create beings whose entire existence is one of endless pain and misery ?

5. How is it possible that from the Eternal there should spring forth finite and temporary beings?

6. Why is the earth round? Why does the moon have no light of its own, but reflects instead the light of the sun? Why is the satellite Telstar round ? Why must the eye contain four colors, with the black segment (the pupil) of the eye serving as the receiving instrument? Why ten fingers and not nine or eleven? In other words, why is any part of this universe created as it is? Is there a set pattern? What does this pattern signify? What does it mean for man?

7. The widespread interest in the occult suddenly appears to have taken a firm hold on a great many people in general, and countless Jews in particular. Why now?

To make all this wholly clear, we must first engage in certain inquiries.

The first inquiry concerns the question of how the creation can be conceived of as being "new" in the sense that something was not contained in the Holy One before He created it.

The second inquiry concerns this: being omnipotent, the Creator can certainly create something from nothing; that is, something that had no existence in Him in any way. Then what is this existence, of which it can be said to have no place within Him, but that which is new.

The third inquiry concerns what the Masters of the Kabbalah have said: that man's soul is part of God on high. This means that there is no difference between Him and the soul, except that He is "the whole" and the Soul is "part". The sages' metaphor for this is a stone hewn from a mountain, there being no difference between the stone and the mountain, save for the one being "part" and the other "the whole". Now we can envisage a stone being separated from the mountain by a suitable tool, by which the "part" is separated from the "whole". But how can we envisage the Holy One, separating a part of His substantiality, which, in turn, becomes a "part" (the Soul) so distinct from it that it can then be conceived as being only a part of His substantiality?

The fourth inquiry is: since the chariot of the Other Side (Evil Forces) and the Husks are so utterly remote from His Holiness that we cannot envisage the distance, how is it possible that it should proceed from, and be brought forth by His Holiness? Furthermore, why is it that His Holiness should even keep it in existence?

The fifth inquiry concerns the Resurrection of the Dead. Since the body is such a contemptible thing, being condemned to die and be buried from the very moment of its birth (the Zohar even says that as long as the body is not entirely decomposed and something of it still remains, the soul cannot ascend to its place in Paradise), therefore, why is it necessary that it should arise again at the Resurrection of the Dead ? Can the Holy One not give pleasure to the soul without it? And even stranger is the saying of our Sages: "The dead will come to life again with all of their infirmities, lest it be said that they are not the same, and then the Holy One will heal their infirmities." We want to understand why it should matter to the Holy One that it might be said that they are different, to the extent that He should have to create their infirmities again and then have to heal them.

The subject of our sixth inquiry is the statement of our sages that man is the center of all existence, and that all the Upper Worlds and this material World have been created only for him. (Zohar Vayikra, 48). The Sages also state in Sanhedrin (37) that the World has been created for him. On the face of it, it is hard to understand that for this little man, who does not account for as much as a hair's worth in the existence of this World, the Holy One should have created all this. Also, why does man need all this?

If we are to understand all these questions and inquiries, we must first consider the purpose of Creation. Nothing can be understood while it is being made, but only after it is completed. And it is clear that there can be no maker without purpose.

Now I know full well that there are would-be scholars (who have thrown off the yoke of the Torah and its Commandments), who say that the Creator created the world and then abandoned it to its fate. The reason for this, they say, is that because of the worthlessness of all creatures, it does not befit the Creator, in all His Exaltation, to watch their despicable ways. But that argument is invalid; for we cannot decide that we are base and worthless unless we decide that we have created ourselves. However, when we decide that the Creator, in His Supreme Perfection, is the artisan who created and designed our bodies, with all the good and evil inclinations inherent in them, it follows then that the perfect Maker can never be said to have turned out despicable, corrupt work.

Is it the fault of a ruined coat that it had been sewn by an inept tailor? This idea is corroborated in Tractate Ta'anith (20), thus:

> **Once Rabbi Elazar, son of Rabbi Shimon, happened to meet a man who was extremely ugly and said to him, "How ugly this man is". Whereupon the ugly man replied: "Go say to the artisan who made me: How ugly is this vessel which you have made."**

Thus, those would-be scholars, who say that

because of our baseness and worthlessness it does not befit the Almighty to watch over us and that He has abandoned us, merely proclaim their own ignorance. Imagine meeting someone to whom it had occurred to create creatures, intended from the first to be plagued and suffer, while they are left to their own devices without any assistance whatsoever. How deeply would you blame and despise him! Is it then conceivable that this would apply to the Holy One, Blessed and Praised Be He?

Thus, common sense leads us to a conclusion that is the opposite of what our first observation seemed to imply. Finally, we must know that we are, in truth, such excellent and exalted creatures that there is no limit to our importance and, therefore, befitting the Artisan who made us. For whatever shortcomings the body seems to possess they only fall back on the Creator who made us with all that is in us by nature. It is obvious that it was He who has made us and not we who have created ourselves; that He also knew all the consequences that would continue to result from all the natural and evil inclinations which he implanted in us. But here, as we have said, we must look to the purpose of the matter, so as to be able to understand.

Our Sages have taught us (see *Etz aim*, "Chapter of the Vessels", 81) that the Holy One has created the world for the purpose of giving enjoyment to those whom He has created. This is what we must attend to with all our thoughts, for this is the purpose of the Creation of the World. Consider this: since the Thought of Creation was to give enjoyment to His creatures, it follows that He created within the Souls an extremely great measure of the "will to receive" what He thought to give them. For the dimension of any pleasure or enjoyment is measured by the dimension of the "will to receive" it. In other words, the greater the "will to receive," the greater the pleasure; the less the "will to receive," the less the pleasure taken in receiving. Hence, the very Thought of Creation requires that the Creation within the soul of the "will to receive" be in exceedingly great measure, for the great enjoyment and the great will to receive are commensurate.

Having learned this, we should then achieve a clear understanding of our second inquiry, regarding the Creation of that which did not exist within the substantiality of the omnipotent Holy One. It follows then that God's thought of Creation, which is to give enjoyment to His creatures, did of necessity create the "will to receive" His good intentions. Thus, we understand that this "will to receive" could certainly not have been contained within His substantiality, for from whom could He have received? Therefore, He created something new that was not within Him. At the same time, it is clear from the Thought of the Creation that there was no need whatsoever to create anything beyond this "will to

Now, when benevolence removed itself, the desire to receive felt a true lack of this benevolence thus causing a real desire to receive which it lacked. This real desire, then, is considered as Phase Four.

These four phases were considered within the very first stage of Creation, meaning "The Endless World," where the desire to receive, manifested as a pure Light, received endlessly from the desire to impart.

At this point, the Kabbalah relates that nothing was lacking, except for the defect experienced by the desire to receive. The Zohar terms this defect whereby the receiver receives constantly without ever benefiting the imparter or giver, as the "Bread of shame". From our experience we know that the constant receiver will eventually begin to resent the hand that feeds him. Now, knowing well that it was the intent of the Creator to impart, the receiver (desire to receive) refused to receive, unless he could reciprocate; for the inevitability of receiving could never be effaced or destroyed, but would have to remain, since this was the reason for Creation.

Thus, through a series of endless changes in the desire to receive, the final manifestation of this desire to receive was the formation of man epitomized by greed. To erase greed man would have to receive and also impart delight (by his acceptance) to the Creator.

Let us assume that one is to receive a fortune of money, which would naturally be welcomed as a result of one's desire to receive. But because of man's ability to control and master his own destiny he refuses to accept purely for the sake of receiving. He then considers this fortunate opportunity as a way to benefit mankind, in that he, in turn, could bestow this wealth upon others. And for this very reason he would accept.

This then is the thought man must have before he can receive: knowing well that the Creator delights in one's acceptance, even though there is the chance of refusal which would be contrary to the Creator's intent, and by accepting on the basis of imparting, the recipient does not feel the "bread of shame". The following analogy clearly illustrates the preceding thought.

A wealthy man in town is about to sit down to a sumptuous meal. Suddenly, peering through a window, he observes a man in rags who obviously has not had a decent meal in days. The rich man invites the poor man in and requests that he partake in the meal. The poor man refuses gently, indicating that he really doesn't need the assistance of the wealthy benefactor. Knowing well that the poor man is in need of a meal and having a desire to do good, he repeatedly insists that the poor man accept his offer. The poor man, although desirous of this meal, refuses because of an innate feeling of "bread of shame." After numerous requests the poor man finally agrees, thereby causing tremendous delight to the wealthy man.

Now what has actually happened here? The wealthy man, the benefactor, suddenly feels he is on the receiving end, and the poor man becomes the imparter, giving delight to the benefactor. We begin to sense a circular feeling running between benefactor and recipient; that is, in receiving there is imparting (the poor man), and with imparting there is receiving (the rich man). This is the cardinal rule of the Kabbalah for one's receiving in any manner or form. In other words, provided there is an element of imparting with the receiving, the receiving is unlimited.

If, however, receiving is merely for oneself, then there is a limit the vessel (the body) may receive, just as a cup limits its contents to the brim of the vessel. But were we to imagine the cup receiving from the outside while imparting simultaneously then there would be limitless receiving.

Essentially, this is the reason for our being: to receive the benevolence of the Creator, but without the element of greed. Therefore, we must condition ourselves so that the Inner Light will have sway over the body (desire to receive); we must remove the limitation of the body, which is, in essence, the factor governing our very existence.

There are three basic governing limitations: time, space and motion. However, within the metaphysical realm, these three components do not exist. How then, can we possibly comprehend metaphysical matters?

The Kabbalah compares a person to a tree in a field, with the tree and its root corresponding to man and his origin. From this we can make important deductions.

We know that a tree is comprised of a root and trunk, branches and fruit, all of which emanate from the root. However, the root shows no sign of its future development. Although within the seed of the tree all future manifestations must exist, nevertheless, we as human beings cannot discern their various future developments. Why? Because the body is composed of the limiting factor of time, space and motion. Thus, as the seed develops in time, space and motion, we visually experience the development. But the limitations need not govern.

Let us take time as a factor. We have all experienced days that either drag or pass swiftly by. How do we explain this? Is time 24 hours in a day?

Let us assume that a man has been placed in a dungeon for a week's time. When he is freed he has absolutely no conception of either what time of the day it is, or how many days have gone by. It is apparent that time is not a governing factor, but more like a basket in which actions are accumulated. Now, if the basket is full of useful accomplishments one feels that the day has gone by quickly. But if the reverse were true, that is, if the basket were empty, one would feel the weightiness of time

The astronauts, for example, have demonstrated to us the dissipation of these limiting factors. In outer space it now takes one and a half hours to traverse the earth, since the factor of gravity is absent. Thus distance is suddenly almost nonexistent — almost to the point of being in two places at the same time! Therefore, it may not require any time or motion to move from one place to another; all will occur almost simultaneously, although, presently, we still cannot discern different concepts contained within one.

We may clarify the problem by recognizing that the final outcome of an act is already present in the thought of that act. This principle applies not only to the thought of Creation, but also to man's thoughts. A multitude of thoughts may go into the accomplishment of any act, yet in the very first thought of an act its finality is already present.

For example, in planning a house, the first thought is the picture of the complete structure.

However, before this is achieved, many details need to be thought out and acted upon. The finished house follows only after many thoughts and many actions. Thus we say that the final act is present in the first thought.

We are taught the simple fundamental idea that by God's thought alone everything was created and brought to its completion. God, however, is not like man, for man must utilize real tools and devices in order for his acts and plans to be materialized. But God's thought, by itself, suffices to complete all acts instantly.

With the concept whereby the body or the limiting factor need not have sway over the Light or Soul, we can now account for ESP, and why it may work between two individuals.

As has been explained, the divisive factor between two souls is the "will to receive." It then follows that, were this factor to be diminished or transmuted to one of imparting, the two individuals may communicate with each other without the aid of any physical means; for we have demonstrated that time, space and motion are the limiting factors, while the body still holds sway over the Light or Soul.

As another example, a physical wall separating two rooms remains as a limiting factor only for those governed by physical elements. Everything existing within Creation is but a photocopy of some form of the "will to receive." Were the particular aspect consisting of the dividing wall removed (metaphysically speaking) the wall would no longer remain as a limiting factor.

With new scientific advances constantly appearing on the scene, the metaphysical concept can be understood. If one had stated some 50 years ago that the noted Kabbalist, Rabbi Isaac Luria, could travel from Safed to Jerusalem within a matter of seconds, there would be little understanding of this seemingly wild statement. Today, however, this can be understood as being possible — if one understands the metaphysical concept.

Furthermore, with a clearer conception of what consists of cause and effect, we may comprehend that the author of the Kabbalah (the Zohar) Rabbi Shimon Bar Yohai, did, in fact, know the exact reason (as opposed to the result of trial and error) why a particular herb would react in a given situation.

Now to the misery and suffering that we all experience in one form or another. This does not (and could not) emanate from the Creator, since He is All Good. From whence does it come? Indirectly, for actions and occurrences are Good, but due to our inabilities in dealing with time, space and motion, they appear to be bad.

Take, for example, the individual who is to conclude a very successful business deal in some distant city and must arrive there with a check at a specific time. For some unknown reason his watch had the wrong time, and upon arrival at the airport, he is told that his plane has just left. Can one imagine the unhappiness and disappointment experienced by this individual? But this condition is short-lived, for upon leaving the airport in his car he tunes in some music on the radio to cheer up his spirits — when suddenly a bulletin comes across the airwaves announcing the crash of the very airplane he was scheduled to be on! No survivors! His mood immediately changes, from feeling distraught to one of relief.

Now how is it possible to experience such greatly different feelings with the same set of events? It is, however, quite obvious that, due to his inability to rise above the limiting factor called time, he could not have visualized the next few moments in time.

It is therefore quite apparent that the governing elements of a "desire to receive" (the "I" and the "Me") are actually the responsible causes of both happiness and unhappiness. Thus, the root of all misery and suffering can be traced to the "will to receive".

Why is the earth round ? To clearly indicate to man his reason for existence, and the reason of his essential being. Man must transmute his "will to receive" to one of imparting so as to create the circular concept whereby giving or imparting enables one to receive endlessly and satisfactorily.

Why is the moon black when not reflecting the light it receives from the sun, thereby demonstrating to man his makeup ? Black represents the epitome of greed, for it has no light of its own. This means that it can only receive before imparting.

Man is constantly engaged in the battle of the pure ("will to impart") verses the impure ("will to receive"). Within all Creation, wherever we may find the concept of evil, therein also lies the manifestation of goodness. There is no element within Creation that does not contain these two basic elements, whether it be an electric current with its positive (imparting) and negative (receiving) charges or the atom.

Therefore, the scientist, without the available Kabbalah knowledge, constructed the Telstar satellite in a circular form via trial and error.[1] Telstar, because it receives messages from without and is circular[2] (indicating the element of imparting), receives and emits endlessly. This is what we call root information or causative-motivation.

1) In a triangular or squared type of construction Telstar could not be effective.
2) It is interesting to find that the Hebrew word "Sfirah" is translated in English as "Sphere".

From the preceding, it becomes obvious why one possesses a left and right hand, as well as why each hand has five fingers: to indicate the four varying degrees of the "will to receive" with its pure and impure source. Therefore, each individual's right hand is somewhat longer, in the hope that his right "will to impart" will extend over his left ("will to receive").

The reason why the eye has four different colors, with the pupil always being black, is to show the four varying degrees of the "will to receive". The pupil, which serves as the actual vessel of receiving, is black because it lacks the ability to impart.

And why is the drug scene so prevalent now? The Kabbalah states that in the time of the Messiah (also known as the "Age of Aquarius") there will occur a tremendous spiritual awakening, the cause of which is the violent revolt of the soul against the governing limitations of the body. For the soul will have had its fill. And the senseless crushing effect of the "I" (will to receive) will be displaced by the love of one's neighbor and consideration for one's friend. This is the root cause for today's "Love" movements; this too is the motivating factor for the drug scene now.

The inner depths of man, call it the subconscious if you will, have been stirred up. Man wants to get away from the insatiable "desire to receive" for oneself, and from the clutches of our limiting factors. For drugs do simulate this experience; and one does become oblivious to his physical surroundings.

However, one thing is wrong. On the return to his present surroundings the individual is back to where he started from. Returning too are his fears, frustrations and inabilities all of which stem from the causative factor, the body ("will to receive"). This is not symptomatic reasoning, changing with time or weather conditions. It may be irrational, but it is not illogical.

Must this violent revolt of the soul manifest itself within our society? Must we experience the violence and conflict throughout the world? or is there some logical method to tame man's self-destructive madness?

This is where the educational process of the Kabbalah will contribute. It is the long sought after conditioning agent that will lead man from his own concerned way of life to recognizing his purpose in being.

Rabbi Philip S. Berg
Editor

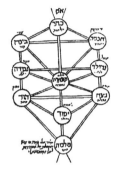

INTRODUCTION

The cave in Piquin, Israel, where the great Kabbalist, Rabbi Shimon Bar Yohai revealed the teachings of the Zohar 2000 years ago.

THIRTEEN YEARS IN A CAVE ... A FATHER and son alone ... and the Zohar took form — the "Book of Splendor", the classic work on the Torah's hidden lore and mysticism.

When Rome ruled Israel, Rabbi Shimon ben Yohai was a disciple of Rabbi Akiva, who had taught Torah despite the persecution of the Romans, until they put him to death. Rabbi Shimon lashed out at the Romans for their evil and cruelty — and Rome sentenced him to death.

Telling no one, he fled with his son Rabbi Elazar to a cave amid the mountains of Israel. They hid there thirteen years until the Roman emperor's death made it safe for them to leave.

Since earliest times there were secret teachings of Divine mysteries in the Torah, that could only interest a few — that only a few enlightened souls could understand. There were texts, mentioned in the Talmud, that originated centuries before. And the Talmud tells of Sages who worked to master such esoteric lore.

The years that Rabbi Shimon ben Yohai spent with his son in the cave marked a turning-point in the history of this great body of hidden knowledge. In the safety of darkness, with no text to read, Rabbi Shimon drew on the deep levels of memory and vision stored in his unconscious from years of study with his masters of the past.

So the Zohar took form — a single work that became the classic text of Kabbalah, the received, transmitted mystic teachings of Judaism. In every generation afterward, a select few guarded it and studied it — until a widespread yearning grew in 14th century Spain for the life-giving teachings of Kabbalah. Then the Zohar became known, to be hidden no more.

Many studied and understood the dazzling truths of Jewish mysticism. But few could make others understand and see. For that, Jewry would have to wait for Safed in the 1500's.

In a small city in Upper Galilee, set on a hill in a lovely mountainous region of Israel, Kabbalah flourished as never before. Jews lived a simple religious life in Safed, supporting themselves, seeking only peace and piety.

There Rabbi Moses Cordovero was born in 1522. Drawn as by a thirst to the wisdom of Kabbalah, he studied with Rabbi Shlomo Alkabetz, author of *L'kha Dodi*, whose sister he married.

In time, Kabbalah found in him what it had long needed: a gifted teacher with a pen. The few works of his that were printed, give the clearest presentation ever made of the main teachings of Jewish mysticism. Through his words in print, the brilliant light of Kabbalah later reached Eastern Europe, to give dynamic life to the great movement of *Hassidut.*

At the same time, Safed had a second master of Kabbalah: Rabbi Isaac Luria, called the Ari.

In his teens the Ari was already a Talmudic authority. Then he discovered the Zohar, and for 13 years he lived as a hermit, plumbing its secrets. In 1569 he settled in Safed, to study briefly with Rabbi Moses Cordovero, until he became a master in his own right, with a devoted circle of disciples.

The Ari could not put his own thoughts down on paper. They were too complex — too filled with rich, interwoven images and allusions, associations and metaphors. But his disciples recorded every possible word and deed, producing the volumes of what we now regard as "his writings."

Although the "writings" were now recorded, nevertheless, the subject matter was to wait till the early 1900's; when a gifted student was to reveal these "writings" intelligibly to the masses.

It started with a modern pioneer — Rabbi

Yehudah Ashlag. A rarely gifted teacher, he could unlock doors for the very beginner; and bring new vision, new awareness in kabbalah's great truths.

At he end of his lifetime on earth, Rabbi Ashlag left three legacies. The first was *HaSulam*, a 21-volume translation-commentary that renders the Zohar from its original abstruse, difficult Aramaic into clear, flowing Hebrew.

His second legacy was *Talmud Eser Sfirot, The Study of Ten Luminous Emanations*, an essential intro-duction to Kabbalah for the novice. No other work of this kind was ever written before. *Talmud Eser Sfirot* consists of 16 volumes. The present publication consists of Volume One, chapters one and two. The writings of the Ari are shown in Hebrew with the English transla-tion in italics, The commentary by Rabbi Ashlag fol-lows under the heading "Inner Light".

The third legacy was his disciple, Rabbi Yehudah Z. Brandwein.

Rabbi Brandwein directed Yeshiva Kol Yehuda (Research Centre of Kabbalah) an academy for the study of the Torah's mysticism, founded by Rabbi Yehudah Ashlag 50 years ago.

With its return to the Walled City of Jerusalem, the

Research Centre of Kabbalah has flowered anew in Israel, in a new period of remarkable growth. There gifted students may learn this lore, in an unbroken tradition that prevailed during the old days of Rabbi Shimon bar Yoai.

In addition, the Research Centre of Kabbalah was founded in the United States to maintain the Academy in Jerusalem, and — more important — to embark on a major, unprecedented program of publications in Hebrew and English.

As a disciple of Rabbi Brandwein and now the Centre's Dean, I have confronted the deeper meaning of the world situation, and, more importantly, I have responded to the cry of our younger generation for knowledge of the reality of existence.

Seminars and lecture series have already commenced. The large and enthusiastic audiences at these lectures have been most gratifying. The Research Centre of Kabbalah has truly contributed to mankind's ability to live in one world without destroying each other.

Rabbi Philip S. Berg

חלק ראשון

צמצום וקו וכולל ב' פרקים

VOLUME ONE

The Tree of Life
Contraction and Line of Light
(Two Chapters)

*Rabbi Yehuda Ashlag, the most profound mystic of
the 20th century, founder of The Kabbalah
Learning Centre in Jerusalem, 1922.*

CHAPTER ONE

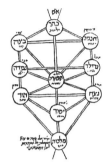

The Tree of Life

Restriction and Line of Light

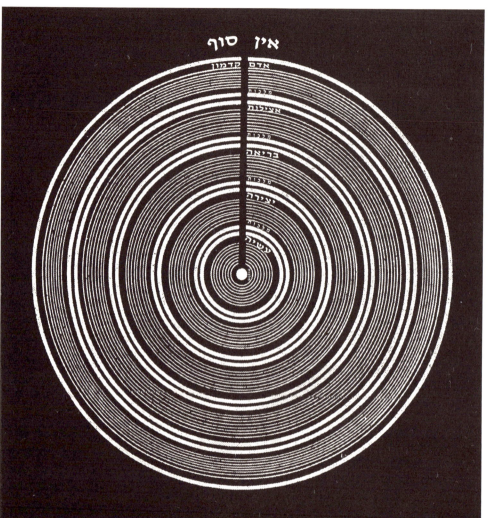

LINE OF LIGHT
AND
ENCIRCLING VESSELS

א) דע כי א טרם שנאצלו הנאצלים ונבראו
הנבראים, היה אור ב עליון פשוט ג ממלא כל
המציאות. ולא היה שום ד מקום פנוי בבחינת
ה אויר ריקני ו וחלל, אלא היה הכל ז ממולא
מן אור א"ס פשוט ההוא, ולא היה ח לו לא
בחינת ראש ולא בחינת סוף, אלא הכל היה
ט אור א' פשוט י, שוה בהשואה א', והוא
הנקרא כ אור א"ס.

1:1

Know that before the emanations were
emanated[1] and the created were created,
the exalted and simple Light[2] had filled
the entire existence,[3] and there was no
empty space[4] whatsoever. As to what may
be called empty air[5] or vacuum,[6] every
thing was filled with that simple and

boundless Light[7] and there was no such part as head,[8] and no such part as tail; that is, there was neither beginning nor end, for everything was one simple Light,[9] evenly spread, in one likeness or affinity[10],and that is called the Endless Light.[11]

I N N E R   L I G H T

We should bear in mind that all the wisdom of Kabbalah is based on spiritual matters, which do not occupy time or space. Disappearance, permutation or change — all are utterly impossible in the spiritual realm. The manifold phases and changes referred to in this wisdom are not meant to convey the idea that the first phase disappeared or assumed a different phase; by "change" we only mean that another phase is added, and the first phase remains as before. Because disappearance or change can occur only within the nature of material objects.

This is the main difficulty for beginners, because they grasp spiritual conceptions in their physical meanings that belong to the limitations of time, space, change and development. Those terms are used by Kabbalists only as symbols that express and reveal their spiritual roots.

Therefore I shall try my best to explain every word in its spiritual concept, divesting it from its physical connotation of time space and change.

It is recommended for the readers to memorize all the explanations presented here.

[1]BEFORE THE EMANATIONS WERE EMANATED   טרם שנאצלו

The concept of spiritual time is thoroughly explained in the coming chapters.

[2]EXALTED LIGHT   אור עליון

This is the Light that extends from the essential being of the Creator. Bear in mind that all the names and appellations discussed in the Wisdom do not, in any way, concern the Creator's essential being, only the Light that extends from Him. For truly speaking, we do not have the slightest idea or expression of his Being.

The general rule is that all that is beyond our conception is beyond our ability to name or define. We recommend that the reader remember this rule so that he may not fail in his understanding.

³HAD FILLED THE ENTIRE EXISTENCE

ממלא כל המציאות

Seemingly there is a contradiction, for we are discussing here a situation in which the world was not created yet, so therefore what sort of reality is there here that needs the filling of the Exalted Light?

The fact of the matter is, all the worlds and all the souls that already exist and those that will be created in the future with all that is to happen to them until their final redemption (or *Tikune*) are already included in the Endless in all their glory and fulfillment, in such a way, that we should distinguish between two main phases in the all- inclusive reality before us:

Period 1: The period of existence in which they exist and are fixed in the Endless in all their glory and perfection.

Period 2: The period of existence where they are arranged in a descending order assuming a new form of five worlds after the first restriction (*Tzimtzum*), these worlds are:

1. The Primordial Man-Archetypal (*Adam Kadmon*)
2. The World of Emanation (*Atziluth*)
3 .The World of Creation (*Briah*)
4. The World of Formation (*Yetzirah*)
5. The World of Action (*Assiah*)

This is what the Ari means when he states: "The Exalted Light had filled the entire existence". That is, the all-inclusive existence in the first phase, where they are set in and exist in the Endless before the Restriction. And he explains that the Exalted Light had completely filled the worlds and souls in such a manner that there was no empty space left that required anything to be added for correction or perfection. In this phase, or period of existence, everything was in its peak of glory, beauty, and perfection.

[4] EMPTY SPACE   מקום פנוי

It means that before the worlds were created, and only the Endless was in existence, there was no "empty space". In other words, there was no lack, so there was no place for the *Tikune* process to be, because the Exalted Light filled this place entirely, in such a manner that it did not allow the lower beings to be able to add anything to Its perfection.

But because of the Restriction (*Tzimtzum*) a new aspect of lack appeared and an empty space for the *Tikune* process was revealed. Nevertheless, we should not be misled to think that the treatise is referring to a physical place.

[5] EMPTY AIR   אויר ריקני

We do not refer to the air of this mundane world, but to that "air" of which earth's atmosphere is only but a copy; there is a sort of spiritual air which assumes the figurative name of "air".

There are two kinds of Light in each and every complete celestial phase (*Partzuf*), which are referred to as the Light of Wisdom and the Light of Grace (Mercy). The Light of Wisdom is the essential being and liveliness of every celestial phase. The Light of Grace is only an enclothing Light for the Light of Wisdom in each phase, because the Light of Wisdom cannot enter each phase if it is not covered or clothed first by the Light of Grace.

Nevertheless, at times when the celestial phases are in a state of "smallness" or contraction, they possess only the Light of Grace. And you should know that this Light of Grace is called Air or Spirit. When it is by itself, without the Light of Wisdom, it is defined by the figurative expression: "empty air". In other words, it is void of Light of Wisdom. Therefore, it yearns for the Light of Wisdom to permeate it and fill it.

That is what the Ari is teaching us, that before the worlds were created in the Endless, there was no state of empty air in being at all, because there is no lack whatsoever, as previously stated.

6 Vacuum   חלל

In order to explain this term, you should know beforehand what is the essential nature and qualities of a spiritual vessel. As the emanated being (the receiver) receives its abundance of liveliness from the Emanator, it is necessary for the vessel to possess the desire and yearning to receive His abundance from Him. And you should know that the extent of this desire and yearning is the full essence of the substance from which the emanated is derived and included within, in such a way, that whatever the emanated beings possess in addition to this substance does not belong to its substantial being. Its substantial being relates to its abundance which is received from the Emanator.

Not only that, but this substance (or spiritual matter) is the rightful measurement of the size (*koma*) of each and every emanated being, *Partzuf* (celestial phase), and *Sfirah*.

Surely, the extension and expansion of the Supernal Light from the Emanator is without any limitation. For it is only the emanated who limits this abundance, because he can accept no more and receive no less than what his desire to receive craves for. This is the actual measurement that is dealt with in the spiritual world. There is no compulsion there, everything depends on the desire.

Thus, we call the desire to receive "the vessel of the emanated". It is considered as its essential substance, and because of it the emanated was severed from the Emanator and came into existence as a separate being. This came to be because there is no desire to receive whatsoever in the Emanator. For how could a desire to receive ever exist in the Emanator, from whom can He ever receive?

We shall further explain that the desire to receive has four stages of development. They proceed from the small, potential and embryonic stage which is the first, up to the fourth stage, which is its final stage and the full capacity of its receiving. This last grade in its complete perfection is found only in the Endless, before the creation of all the worlds.

Only this desire to receive, in its complete perfection in the Endless, underwent the mystery of Restriction. So the "desire" became empty of all the abundance it received from the Endless. As shall be discussed further, when the desire became empty of all the infinite abundance it received in the Endless, it remained "void" or empty space.

7 Filled with that Simple and Boundless Light   ממולא מן אור א"ס

That is to say, nothing whatsoever could be added to, or placed within, by actions or deeds of this world.

8 No Such Part as Head   לא בחינת ראש

The matter of head or tail will be explained in later chapters.

9 One Simple Light   אור א' פשוט

This means that there are no shades of clarity (purity) or density of the stages to be arranged.

10 EVENLY SPREAD IN ONE LIKENESS AND AFFINITY

שׂוה בהשואה א'

This means that there are no shades of clarity (purity) or density (impurity) of the phases to be arranged, because all the phases of the worlds came into existence only after the Restriction.

11 THE ENDLESS LIGHT

אור א"ס

We have no conception whatsoever of the Endless. So we may ask, how can we define it? A definition means that we are able to grasp it, and the name of an object indicates our understanding of it.

The answer lies in the word "Endless" itself, because the name "Endless" shows our inability to grasp it. If that is the case why don't we call it inconceivable? The fact of the matter is that this name "endless" does show us the difference between the endless state of being and the state of the worlds beyond.

That is because of the Restriction. Every time this action occurs, it restricts the Light, and thus the Light expands no more and reaches an end. Therefore every end that is located in every Illumination and every *Sfirah* is revealed only because of the Restriction. Not only that but because of this state of Endless, all the new states of being and their developments are brought forward.

Because there is no Restriction in the Endless, there is no end there. That is why it is called "Endless". Now we can understand that the Light is simple and has no degrees of large or small.

ב) וכאשר׳ עלה ברצונו הפשוט, לברוא
העולמות ולהאציל הנאצלים, להוציא לאור
שלימות פעולותיו ושמותיו וכינויו, אשר זאת
היה סיבת בריאת העולמות.

1:2

And from within His simple desire arose the will[12] to create the worlds and to manifest the emanations, to bring to light the perfection of His deeds and His names and His appellations which was the reason for the creation of the worlds.

I N N E R   L I G H T

12 FROM WITHIN HIS SIMPLE DESIRE AROSE THE WILL

עלה ברצונו הפשוט

It may be surprising to find desire in the Endless which is beyond any human ability to grasp. But we should understand that in each and every emanated being there must be a desire to receive the abundance from the Emanator. In the Endless this desire is "Simple", as is conveyed in the veiled words: "He is One and His Name is One".

As stated in Chapter One of Rabbi Eliezer the Great, the Light of the Endless is referred to as "He", while the desire to receive which must necessarily exist in the Endless is symbolized by the words "His Name". Both expressions, "He and His Name", represent a simple and absolute Unity; There is no separation whatsoever between them.

However, we must not conclude that the terms Unity and Separation mentioned here resemble the same terms in the physical realm. Physical matter is separated by motion and distance, while spiritual essence does not take up any space at all.

We should know that separation in spiritual entities occurs by "transformation" from one phase to another. This transformation happens by "differentiation of form" only.

If a spiritual entity happens to acquire another form of existence different from its original one, it has transformed from one simple phase to two different phases. These two forms are as far from each other as the extent of the diversity between them.

Just as physical matter is separated by distance and unified by closeness, spiritual entities are separated by dissimilarity and are unified by similarity. Please remember this, because it is the main key to the Wisdom of Kabbalah.

We should now be able to understand the veiled meaning of the words: "He and His Name are One", and the expression of simple and absolute Unity that we refer to so accurately in the Endless. This unity is one of His great marvels, revealing the most wondrous and astonishing quality in Him.

The difference between the Emanator and the emanated, which came into being because of the desire to receive that exists in the emanated but not in the Emanator, caused the emanated to have a different name than the Emanator.

By that we may be misled into thinking that the Endless Light, referred to as "He" is not in complete Unity (*Dvekut*) with the Endless, referred to as "His Name". By the term "His name" we mean the desire to receive the abundance and the Light which is called "He". Because the Exalted Light — "He" — which is drawn from the essential Being of the Creator, has only one desire and that is to share, and has no desire to receive whatsoever.

This is not the case in the Endless — "His Name" — that has the desire to receive and is different therefore from the Exalted Light.

As we already know, dissimilarity of form causes separation between entities. Nevertheless, that is what Rabbi Eliezer the

Great, and the Ari, are explaining to us that "He" and "His Name" are completely and fully unified, and there is no difference between them whatsoever.

Even though there is some dissimilarity between "He" and "His Name", in any case it does not exist there (in the Endless) at all.

Although we are not able to grasp this paradox, we know beyond any doubt that that is how it is. That is why it is said that the Endless is far beyond the grasp of human intellectual powers.

ג) והנה אז מ צמצם את עצמו א"ס נ בנקודה
האמצעית, אשר בו באמצע ממש, וצמצם
האור ההוא, ס ונתרחק אל ע צדדי סביבות
הנקודה האמצעית.

1:3

And behold the Endless restricted
Himself,[13] in the central point within
Him,[14] precisely in the center, and this
restricted the Light, and the Light withdrew[15] towards the sides around the central point.[16]

I N N E R   L I G H T

13 RESTRICTED HIMSELF   צמצם את עצמו

We already know the inner meaning of the words "He and His Name are One". That even though there is a difference of form (dissimilarity) in the state of being of the desire to receive that is included in the Endless, in any case there is no separation whatsoever between it and the Exalted Light. They are in a state of complete unity. Nevertheless the matter of form as explained is the reason and cause of creating all the worlds; to reveal the perfection of His deeds, names and appellations.

The creation of the worlds gave space for divine service by the precepts of the Torah. Not for the purpose of meriting a reward, but for the sole purpose of imparting delight and satisfaction to the Creator. By this, the souls are able to transform the desire to receive that separates them from the Creator, to the desire of sharing (which resembles the desire of the Creator), in order to attain the highest degree of devotion and unity.

As the stage of unity is attained, the souls become altruist instead of egoist, and are able to reach complete resemblance with the Creator.

That is the meaning of the verse "from within His simple desire arose." "Arose", meaning there was an arousal in purification and unity — by reducing and restricting the amount of the desire to receive engraved in Him in order to reach resemblance to the Exalted Light. And even though the desire to receive in the

Endless known as "*Malkhut* of the Endless" or the "Kingdom of the Endless" was in complete unity with the Exalted Light, nevertheless it "decorated" itself by arousing the desire to share in order to reach resemblance with the Exalted Light; also to rid Itself of the great desire to receive in It which is called "His Name" or the "Fourth Phase".

That is what is meant by the word "arose" meaning that the "Kingdom of the Endless" or the "simple desire" became unified with the Exalted Light. In other words — It restricted Its desire to receive — as previously stated.

By the verse "restricted Himself" Rabbi Isaac Luria means that while all the size and proportion of the emanated is measured according to the desire to receive within Him, when the "Kingdom of the Endless" restricted Itself and reduced the desire to receive, the Light withdrew. And with it all the abundance that was in this desire.

This is the whole content of Restriction: the arousal of the desire caused the withdrawal of the Light.

14 IN THE CENTRAL POINT WITHIN HIM   נקודה אמצעית אשר בו

This may seem quite surprising, for if there is no head or tail, how can a central point exist? Especially if we are dealing in spiritual existence and not physical matter.

Nevertheless, the fact remains that even in the Endless there is a desire to receive, but it is a "simple desire". Meaning, that there are no different grades or levels of desire. There is no smallness or largeness of desire to receive that may cause any dissimilarity or separation from the Exalted Light or any inferiority towards It.

We should know, that the Exalted Light must go through four grades before it reveals in the emanated the desire to receive in its full and permanent form.

The reason for the existence of four grades is as follows: The desire to receive is included immediately and simultaneously with the expansion of the Light from the source. By this we perceive the difference between the Light and the Emanator, (the Source). The expansion of the Light in that manner enabled it to acquire a name of its own. And as long as there is no dissimilarity in form caused by the desire to receive in it, it is still considered to be the Emanator, and not the expansion from Him. Because in the spiritual realm there is no difference among beings unless there is dissimilarity in form.

And as long as there is no revelation of this desire by the emanated himself, it is not established permanently in him yet. In other words, the emanated has to crave to receive the abundance. For then we are able to perceive that the desire to receive has been aroused by the emanated on his own initiative.

This craving cannot be revealed except when the emanated has no abundance. Because only then is the craving considered to arouse the "desire to receive" in its full complete and permanent form.

Furthermore, we should know, that every extension of Light from the Emanator, including the desire to receive, must include the desire to impart as well. Because if it weren't so, the Emanator and the emanated would be separated from each other as two different poles.

That is why it is necessary that the Light extended from the Emanator should include the desire to impart as well, so that it may not lose its similarity and affinity with the Emanator.

For when this desire to impart is aroused in the emanated, a great Light is drawn towards it from the Emanator, because of this arousal. The Light is referred to always as the Light of Mercy or Grace. While the first extension from the Emanator, in which the desire to receive is already included within, is called the Light of Wisdom or the Light of Essence.

The second Light, or the Light of Mercy, is inferior in quality compared to the first Light, the Light of Wisdom, because the Light of Mercy is drawn by the arousal of the emanated on its own, due to its desire to reach affinity with the Creator by arousing the desire to impart, as previously explained.

That is not the case in the first extension, which is the Light of Wisdom, which is drawn directly from the Emanator. And the emanated has no part whatsoever in It's revelation. That is why it is greatly superior to the Light of Mercy.

Therefore, the Light of Wisdom is considered to be the essential being and vitality of the emanated, while the Light of Mercy is perceived only as the Light, which prepares the emanated to reach its full and complete form.

We shall explain now the four phases and grades that necessarily must be in each and every emanated being. Firstly, the Light extends from the Emanator and forms the Light of Wisdom, in which only the "desire to receive" is included within — this is the first phase. After that, the desire to impart is aroused in this Light and draws forth the Light of Mercy. This arousal is considered to be the second phase. Then the Light of Mercy is greatly expanded, (this will be further explained) as the third phase is reached. And now, after all three phases have been completed, the power of the desire to receive which is included in the first extension draws down again the Light of Wisdom. And this is the completion of establishing the desire to receive in each celestial phase or entity (*Partzuf*).

The revelation is complete because of the craving, which means when there was no Light of Wisdom in the *Partzuf* (emanated being) but only Light of Mercy — that is after the three phases, when the emanated craved to receive the Light of Wisdom. This craving determines the desire to receive and completes the vessel of receiving in the emanated being.

This was not the case in the first extension. Therefore the vessel of receiving is not completed until the fourth phase, which is also called the second arousal. And after the completion of this fourth phase in the Endless the restriction came into place. The desire to receive departed from this fourth phase and caused the withdrawal of the Endless Light from it.

At this point, the four phases that necessarily have to be in each and every emanated being have been thoroughly explained and can be summed up as follows:

1. The first phase is the first extension (of the Light) known as Wisdom (*hochma*).

2. The second phase is the first arousal (of the vessel) known as Intelligence (*Binah*).

3. The third phase is the second extension (of the Light) known as "Small Face" (*Zeir Anpin*).

4. The fourth phase is the second arousal (of the vessel) known as Kingdom (*Malkhut*).

The two extensions are considered "masculine" because they consist of the abundance drawn from the Emanator. The first extension is the abundance of the Light of Wisdom, and the second extension is the abundance of the Light of Mercy.

While the two arousals are considered "female", because they represent the arousal of the emanated being on his own behalf. The first arousal is of the desire to impart in the emanated which is the source of the Light of Mercy. And the second arousal is of the desire to receive in the emanated, which forms the vessel of receiving of the *Partzuf* in all its desirable completion. It is always referred to as the fourth phase.

The fourth phase is called the "Central Point of the Endless". That is the intended meaning of the Ari when he said that He restricted Himself in the Central Point "within Himself". It is called so because it is a vessel of recipiency for the Endless Light, which is beyond any measurement or limitation at all. That is why it is considered as though it is in the center of this Light, in such a manner that the Light encircled it endlessly and is united with it completely. Only in this way, can it behold within itself the infinite Exalted Light.

This is not the case after the Restriction (*Tzimtzum*) in the lower emanated beings, who contain the Light in the vessels of desire to receive. For they contain the Light in the interior side of the vessel.

In other words, the walls of the vessels (the four phases), form a limitation on the ability to contain the Light in them, due to their thickness (impurity). But in the Endless the Light and the vessel are in complete unity: "He and His Name are One". Therefore the vessel does not limit the entrance of the Light at all. That is why the Light within it is infinite (Endless).

We have now a full description of the "Central Point" in the Endless. We do not mean any physical place, as when we speak of a tangible object perceptible to our senses. But we refer only to the fourth phase included within the Endless which is called the "Central Point", because of its capacity to hold the Light of the Infinite and be in complete unity with It.

¹⁵AND THE LIGHT WITHDREW   ונתרחק

Spiritual distance has been explained earlier. It has already been explained, that in the Endless there is no distance between the Central Point, the vessel, and the Light. But as the Light withdrew from the Central Point, it revealed the dissimilarity between them, because the Light has no desire to receive at all. The Central Point is considered to be the "Desire to Receive" which is different from the Light. Because of this dissimilarity, they are as distant from each other as the dissimilarity between them.

16 SIDES AROUND THE CENTRAL POINT · סביבות הנקודה האמצעית

The four grades mentioned before refer to the four sides as well. Rabbi Isaac Luria informs us that even though the Restriction was only within the realm of the Central Point, the fourth grade, in any case the Light withdrew from all the four grades completely and at once. There is no gradual appearance or disappearance in spiritual reality.

Gravesite of the great Kabbalist, Rabbi Isaac Luria,
The Ari, in Safed, Israel.

ד) ואז נשאר: פ מקום פנוי, ואויר, וחלל ריקני,
מנקודה האמצעית ממש. והנה צ הצמצום
הזה, היה בהשואה א' בסביבות הנקודה
האמצעית ריקנית ההיא, באופן שמקום החלל
ההוא, היה ק עגול מכל סביבותיו בהשואה
גמורה, ולא היה כתמונת מרובע בעל זוית
נצבת, לפי, שגם א"ס צמצם עצמו בבחינת
עגול, בהשואה א' מכל הצדדים.

1:4

And there remained an empty space,
atmosphere, and a vacuum,[17] surrounding
the exact central point. And behold this
Restriction was equally balanced[18] around
the central point in such a manner that
the empty space was circular in shape
from all directions. It was not in the
shape of a cube which has straight
angles.

The Endless also restricted Himself in a circular form equally on all sides[19] **because the Endless Light has no grada-tions. Therefore, the Restriction occurred equally from all sides.**

INNER LIGHT

[17]**AN EMPTY SPACE, ATMOSPHERE, AND A VACUUM.**

מקום פנוי
ואויר וחלל ריקני

See Chapter One, Reference Number 4.

[18]**THIS RESTRICTION WAS EQUALLY BALANCED**

הצמצום הזה היה בהשוואה

This means that there were no distinguishable grades — small or large. But, we might ask, if there is no similarity of the

Central Point with the Light, because of It's withdrawal, then obviously the grades or levels should be different in size.

For example, the third grade is purer than the fourth grade (Central Point), because its desire to receive is smaller. And the second grade is purer than the third grade and would therefore have a smaller desire to receive. The first grade is the purest of them all because it has the smallest desire to receive of them all. That is why the dissimilarity with the Light in the first grade is hardly felt as compared with the other grades.

So we can see that the four levels each have a different size of desire to receive, so how can the Ari say that the Restriction was equally balanced from all sides of the Central Point?

The answer lies in the fact that the Restriction did not cause the Central Point to become an "End". In other words, if the Light had withdrawn from the Central Point because of its dissimilarity with the Light, then of course it could come to an "end". Which means, it would have reached the lowest grade possible. And then the other three grades would have been considered superior to it, in a gradual form.

But this was not the case, as the Restriction did not occur because of dissimilarity with the Light. We should bear in mind that we are still dealing with the *Malkhut* of the Endless, and there is no difference at all between it and the Light. They are in a state of complete unity, according to the meaning of the verse "He and His Name are One".

The Restriction occurred in the arousal of His simple desire to create the worlds (see Inner Light 13). The vessel desired to reach that similarity with the Light that was meant to be revealed by the creation of the worlds. That is, a form of receiving for the sake of imparting. There is in that a highest quality. From one point of view this is complete sharing because the entire desire is only to bestow joy and delight to the Creator and nothing for the needs of one's self alone. And that is why this form is the complete similarity with the Exalted Light.

On the other hand this enables Him to enlarge and deepen the vessel of recipiency up to the level of Endless receiving. Because now the desire to receive causes no dissimilarity with the Light anymore, as it comes from the desire to impart.

A good example of this is found in the Talmud (Tractate *Kidushin*, p.7). According to the Mosaic Law, the man is required to present a wedding ring to the bride. By handing it to the bride, she becomes his legal bride.

The Talmud, however, describes an odd event which is entirely contrary to the previously stated law. In this case it is the woman who hands the money or the wedding ring, and the man cites the verse, "You shall by this become betrothed to me ...". And they are legally married.

This is explained by the fact that when a man of high esteem receives a betrothal gift of money or a ring it is considered that he is sharing his esteem with her and consequently the act of receiving is considered as giving.

That is why the main reason for the restriction is the great desire to reach the state of receiving in order to impart, which was to be achieved once the worlds were created. And not because there was any impurity of density in the spiritual substance in the Central Point. There was no dissimilarity to the Light whatsoever, that may cause it to reach a state of "end", as a result of the Restriction. That is why there is no distinction between large or small at all. This is the intention of the Ari when he says: "equally balanced".

19 EQUALLY ON ALL SIDES   עגול מכל סביבותיו בהשוואה

Because of the Restriction an image of some sort appeared, even though it occurred equally on all sides. But as it caused the Light to withdraw, it came to be that the Central Point and the Light couldn't remain in perfect unity because of the great desire to receive in it. And because this state was revealed, the Central Point fell to a state more inferior than it was in the Endless. It was reduced from the Endless state of being and came to an "end", a limited state of being. Which means it reached the greatest density in its spiritual form.

Only the Central Point became an empty space, and was not worthy anymore to receive the Light. While the other three phases which didn't reach the greatest density form, were still worthy to contain the Light, even after the Restriction.

The empty space was circular in shape from all directions. This means there was no "end" or limit, but rather an "end" that is found at the exact center of a circle.

We may picture the four phases as four circles one inside the other, just like the layers of an onion. The innermost circle may be considered as the fourth phase (Central Point) surrounded by another circle — the third phase. Which is also surrounded by another circle — the second phase. And the first phase surrounding it.

That's how there's no up or down, left or right between them. For example, the upper half of the first phase encircles all the others from above, while the lower half from below. And the same applies to all the other phases. That is why there is no "above or beneath", "right" or "left". No one of them excels the other. All phases are in a state of complete unity and equality.

ה) והסבה היתה, לפי שכיון שאור הא"ס שוה
בהשואה גמורה הוכרח נ"כ, שיצמצם עצמו
בהשואה א' מכל הצדדים, ולא שיצמצם עצמו
מצד א' יותר משאר צדדים. ונודע בחכמת
השיעור שאין תמונה כל כך שוה כמו ר תמונת
העיגול, משא"כ, ש בתמונת מרובע בעל זוית
נצבת בולטת, וכן ת תמונת המשולש וכיוצא
בשאר התמונות. וע"כ מוכרח הוא להיות
צמצום הא"ס בבחינת עיגול.

1:5

It is well known in geometry that a sphere
or circle is the most balanced and uni-
form figure. This is not the case with the
cube[20] or the triangle,[21] because of their
angular form. So, the Restriction had to
be in a circular form. After the
Restriction, there was a Line withdrawn
from the Endless, gradually into the
empty space.

²⁰ THE CUBE   תמונת מרובע

If there were an ability to distinguish between directions as above and below or right and left, we would have to picture a cubical form in the Endless. But that is not the case, the Restriction was in a circular form completely balanced from all directions.

²¹ THE TRIANGLE   תמונת המשולש

This form relates to a phase in the creation process that has only three grades, with a fourth excluded. The three grades are: up, right and left (the fourth direction "down" is missing). This is called the triangular form.

CHAPTER TWO

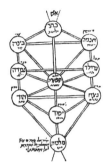

THE TREE OF LIFE

RESTRICTION AND LINE OF LIGHT

The private room in the synagogue of Rabbi Isaac Luria, The Ari, where he taught Kabbalah to his student, Rabbi Chaim Vital in the 16th century.

א) וְהִנֵּה אַחַר הַצִּמְצוּם הַנַּ"ל, א אֲשֶׁר אָז
נִשְׁאַר מְקוֹם הֶחָלָל וַאֲוִיר פָּנוּי וְרֵיקָנִי בְּאֶמְצַע
אוֹר הָא"ס מַמָּשׁ כַּנַּ"ל, הִנֵּה כְּבָר הָיָה מָקוֹם
שֶׁיּוּכְלוּ לִהְיוֹת שָׁם הַנֶּאֱצָלִים וְהַנִּבְרָאִים
וְהַיְצוּרִים וְהַנַּעֲשִׂים. וְאָז ב הִמְשִׁיךְ מִן אוֹר
הָא"ס, קַו אֶחָד יָשָׁר ג מִן הָאוֹר הָעִגּוּל שֶׁלּוֹ
ד מִלְמַעְלָה לְמַטָּה, וּמִשְׁתַּלְשֵׁל, וְיוֹרֵד תּוֹךְ
הֶחָלָל הַהוּא.

2:1

And herewith, after the Restriction, there remained an empty space and a void[22] in the middle of the Endless Light. And already, there became space for the emanated and created beings. Then, one Straight Line was drawn[23] from His Circular Light[24] It descended gradually from above downwards[25] into the empty space.

I N N E R   L I G H T

22 AN EMPTY SPACE AND A VOID   אחר הצמצום

Don't be misled, there was no change of form in the Central Point of the Endless. There can be no change or lack in the spiritual realm, especially in such an elevated and high form of existence.

The Restriction was an addition to the Endless state of being in such a way that the Endless remained in it's complete unity just as it was before the Restriction occurred as described in the verse: "He and His Name are One."

The Restriction that occurred in the Central Point caused a new world, a state of being, to appear. From this world the Light was withdrawn and there was empty space instead, in which all the worlds were emanated.

23 THEN ONE STRAIGHT   המשיך מאור א"ס קו אחד
LINE WAS DRAWN

We should not relate our understanding of this verse to simple human functioning. As though a deed had been started in such a way and then changed to a different way. For the Creator is far beyond our limited and physical conceptions. He is not subject to the changes of our physical existence. As stated: "I, God, do not change ... ". אני הוי' לא שניתי וכו'

Furthermore, we are not here discussing the Creator's essential being, only the Light that extends from Him. In any case, there is no change, movement, or development in Him at all, for He is in absolute rest.

Therefore, this must apply to the Light that extends from Him as well, because as long as the Light did not reach the state of an emanated being, which means enclothed in a vessel, the Light is considered unified with the Creator.

Only when the Light leaves the Essential Being of the Creator and becomes part of the vessel does the new world come into being.

This new existence is due mainly to the vessel, because of its "desire to receive". Even though this desire is spiritual, nevertheless it is considered as a new form of existence — an incidental event.

There are no incidental events in the Creator's Being and the Light which is united with Him. The appearance of the Light is not considered to be a new event. Because its existence comes already from an existing Being — the Creator.

This is not the case when the Light is extended towards the emanated being. Because then the vessel receives the Light and is affected by it. This effect, which is caused by the vessel is an "incidental" event, and has its implication on the Light as well.

You should know that all the new appearances and the gradual descending of all the phases of the creation concern only the vessels reaction towards the receiving of the Light, for only the vessel is subject to the manifold diversities and conditions of expansion and increase. The Light is always in a state of absolute rest. This tranquility is derived from It's origin — the Creator.

By what has been already explained, you should understand thoroughly, that the Exalted Light does not cease to emanate its benevolence to the emanated beings at all, and is not affected by any incidental events or new developments. The Light is always in a state of complete rest and all the events of the Restriction and the withdrawal of the Light mentioned concern only the reaction of the vessel and its desire to receive, the Central Point.

In other words, even though the Exalted Light did not cease to shine upon the emanated beings, the vessel did not receive anything from It's benevolence, because it restricted itself.

With the other three phases the desire to receive is much weaker than the desire that is related to the fourth phase of the vessel which is the Central Point itself. Therefore the other three phases are considered as having a greater desire to share than that of the fourth phase.

That's how the Exalted Light was not affected at all by the Restriction, and did not change It's state of being at all. Just as It shone in the Endless, It continued to shine during the Restriction and after it, including all the worlds even in the World of Action, never ceasing even for a moment. It is the vessels themselves which cause all the changes, by not receiving except to the extent of their "desire to receive".

This explains the Ari's statement: "A Line was drawn from the Endless". Which means the empty space or vacuum, or in other words the vessel that was emptied from the Endless Light. This was caused by the Restriction of the "Desire to Receive", a new event in itself.

The capacity of the desire of the fourth phase after the restriction is called the Line. Before the restriction the capacity to receive for the fourth phase was the whole space which was full. After the restriction it doesn't have this great desire to receive, it has only the other three phases in which the desire to receive is smaller. Therefore it is considered that this vessel is receiving from the Endless Light only a Line of Light, while all the space of the vessel remains empty and void of the Light. This dim Light that the vessel is receiving now is not enough to fill all the space in the vessel. This new state has been caused by the restriction of the fourth phase.

And as previously stated, the Exalted Light did not cease to shine because of the Restriction and did not change because of it, to be drawn down in a form of Line. The new appearance and the great change that occurred when the vessel restricted in that manner, resulted in the vessel receiving from the Endless Light only a small amount of what is called the Light. In other words, according to the capacity of its desire; that is, the vessel wouldn't want any more than that.

24 FROM HIS CIRCULAR LIGHT   מן האור העגול שלו

The meaning of the symbolic term, Circular Light, has been previously explained. It stresses the fact that even after the Restriction the Exalted Light remained in a circular form, without any sides or gradation. All four grades are equally meritorious as far as the Light is concerned. This is so because any new event or incident does not affect the Light, and the manifold mutations which have been mentioned, concern the vessels alone.

25 FROM ABOVE DOWNWARDS   מלמעלה למטה

Do not forget that the meaning intended by the Ari does not refer to physical conceptions. But rather the meaning is that the superior and purer grade is called "above" while the lower and thicker grade is considered to be "below".

And all that can be understood by the extension of the Light from the Emanator and becoming an emanated being, is that mainly a new form of being was caused by the dissimilarity from the Light; in other words, the desire to receive has newly appeared in it that does not exist in the Emanator. And because of that, the emanated being is considered to be afar, thick, and insignificant, compared to the Emanator. The dissimilarity between them causes all these to appear and separate the Emanator from the emanated.

This dissimilarity of form, the desire to receive, is not revealed at once. It is formed gradually, according to the four grades and is completed in the fourth grade, where the amplified and most complete form of desire is manifested.

We can see now, that as the *grade* of the desire to receive is higher and in a weaker form, referring to the first grade among the four, it is considered to be closest to the

Emanator. It is more important and purer, because the dissimilarity of form in it is not as intense as it appears in the other three grades.

While the second grade, in which the desire to receive is greater than the first grade, is considered to be further from the Emanator because it is thicker, lower, and less significant compared to the first grade. Until we reach the fourth grade, which is the furthest from the Emanator, thickest, lowest, and the least significant.

This is what the Ari means when he says that the Line was drawn from "above downwards". In other words, from the first grade down to the fourth one (the last one is not included), which is the lowest of them all.

The subject of "above and below" has newly appeared with the revelation of the Line. Before the Line had appeared, before the Restriction, there was no above or below. When the Light made a new appearance, as the Line, which means that It shone only in the first three grades, and the fourth grade remained empty and dark without the Light, only then is the fourth grade revealed as the lowest and the thickest of them all. And because of this revelation, the other three grades appear to be clearer, purer, and closer to the Emanator.

This was not the case during the Restriction. When the Light disappeared from all four grades at once there was no separation between the grades at all.

ב) ה וראש העליון של הקו, נמשך מן הא"ס
עצמו, ונוגע בו, אמנם סיום הקו הזה, למטה
בסופו אינו נוגע באור א"ס.

2:2

The upper head[26] of the Line was extended from the Endless, Himself, and it con-
tacted Him.[27]

ג) ודרך הקו הזה נמשך ונתפשט אור א"ס למטה.

2:3

Actually, the end of that Line below did
not contact the Endless Light[28].

I N N E R L I G H T

26 THE UPPER HEAD   ראש עליון

This refers to the first of the four grades, as outlined above.

27 AND IT CONTACTED HIM   ונוגע בו

The first grade, which is considered to be the upper head, is the closest to the Endless, the Emanator. Therefore it is said that it touches Him, as there is no dissimilarity in the form of desire to separate it from the Emanator.

28 THE END OF THAT   למטה בסופו אינו נוגע באור א"ס
LINE BELOW DID NOT
CONTACT THE ENDLESS LIGHT

"Below" refers to the fourth grade, which is the furthest of them all and the lowest. It does not receive the Exalted Light, and therefore it is said that it does not touch the Light of the Endless, but is separated from Him.

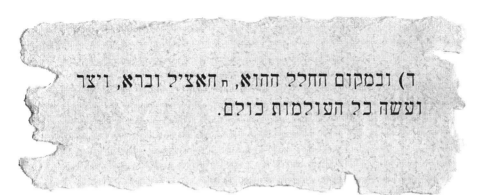

ד) וּבִמְקוֹם הֶחָלָל הַהוּא, ‏ה‏ הֶאֱצִיל וּבָרָא, וְיָצַר
וְעָשָׂה כָּל הָעוֹלָמוֹת כֻּלָּם.

2:4

Through this Line, the Light of the
Endless is drawn, and it extends down-
ward. In this space He emanated, created,
formed and made[29] all the worlds.

I N N E R   L I G H T

29 **EMANATED, CREATED,**   האציל וברא ויצר ועשה
FORMED AND MADE.

This refers to the four worlds:

Atziluth	World of Emanation	אצילות
Briah	World of Creation	בריאה
Yetzirah	World of Formation	צירה
Assiah	World of Action	עשיה

They include all the worlds that are so many that they
cannot be counted. And these four worlds extend from the four
grades: The World of Emanation from the first grade; the World
of Creation from the second grade; the World of Formation from
the third grade; and the World of Action from the fourth grade.

ה) ט קודם הד' עולמות אלו, היה האַ"ס,
הוא אחד ושמו אחד באחדות נפלא ונעלם
ית', כ שאָין כח אפילו במלאכים הקרובים
אליו ואַין להם השגה באַ"ס ית', כי אַין שום
שכל נברא שיוכל להשיגו, להיות, כי י אַין
לו מקום ולא גבול ולא שם.

2:5

Prior to the four worlds,[30] the Endless was
in a state of "He is One and His name is
One",[31] in a wondrous concealed unity, for
there is no ability even in the Angels
above who are close to Him to conceive
the Endless, Blessed be He. There is no
created mind that can grasp Him, since
He is beyond the limitations of space
and definitions of name.

(The Gates of the Sages, Sabbath)

INNER LIGHT

30 PRIOR TO THE FOUR WORLDS.   קודם חד' עולמות הוא ושמו אחד

Which are called: Emanation, Creation, Formation, and Action, and they include all the worlds.

Before these worlds appeared, before the Restriction, there was no upper or lower in these four grades. They were in complete unity. Without any difference between the grades or between the Light and the Vessel. As is stated in the verse, "He is One and His Name is One".

31 HE IS ONE AND HIS NAME IS ONE.   הוא אחד ושמו אחד

"He" points to the concept of the Exalted Light, while "His Name" represents the phase of the will to receive, which inevitably exists there.

His Name, *Shmo* שמו, whose numerical value is 346, is also equal to the numerical value of *Ratzon* רצון or "desire", whose value is also 346. This indicates that "His Name" and "desire" are numerically equal and are both connected to the same meaning — "the desire to receive".

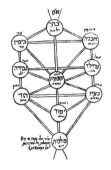

INNER REFLECTION

WE SHOULD FIRSTLY KNOW, THAT WE ARE DEALING WITH spiritual matters and that these matters are beyond the limitations of time, space, and motion. Moreover when we are dealing with divine essence we hardly possess the words to express ourselves, for all our words and ideas are taken from the experiences of our limited senses. How can we use them in a place where the senses and the imagination do not govern?

For example, even if we consider the word "Light". It is also borrowed from the light of the sun or "light", meaning a feeling of being satisfied or joyful. How can we express divine matters when our limited language won't offer the reader the truth of the matter.

Therefore the sages of the Kabbalah chose a special language that may be called the "Language of Branches", which is based on the fact that everything we have in this world is derived from its source or root in the upper world. Not only that, but the beginning of every existing entity in the mundane world, starts from the upper world and later descends to this one.

So the Kabbalists found a suitable language with which they were able to communicate with each other and inform about their revelations. This was done orally and in writing from generation to generation, by using the names of the "branches" in this world, where each name is understood to refer to its upper root in the system of the upper worlds.

Knowing this, your mind should be at ease when you find in Kabbalistic books surprising expressions strange to the human mind. The reason is that they have chosen this language to express themselves. How can they omit any branch and not use it because of its abstruse meaning and thereby not express the desired idea at all.

At the same time, we won't find in our world any other branch that we can use instead. There are no two hairs that grow from one follicle, there are no two branches that are connected to the same root.

It is a loss to omit any part of this wisdom because of the difficulty of expression. Not only that but this omission and loss would cause great confusion in all of this great wisdom.

If we compare this wisdom to other kinds of worldly wisdom we already know, we shall find that there is no other wisdom like the Kabbalah where all the subjects are so connected to each other in a manner of cause and effect. Just like a chain, every link is connected to the other from the beginning to the end. So there is no place for changing arbitrarily.

We must always use the exact branch that refers to its upper root, and explain it as thoroughly as possible until we find the exact meaning before presenting it to the reader.

For those who haven't merited the spiritual understanding of heavenly matters, and are not familiar with the relation of the branches in this world with their roots in the upper worlds, they are like the blind, groping in the dark. They won't know one word of its true meaning, as every word is a name of some branch that is related to its root, unless they receive the meaning from a well-known Kabbalist who presents himself as a person who is able to explain these matters in the spoken language, since he is translating from one language to another, in other words, from the "language of the branches" to the spoken language. In this way, he is able to explain the spiritual terms. שפת הענפים

This is the reason why I am trying to explain the Ten Luminous Emanations as we were taught by our divine teacher, the holy Ari (Rabbi Isaac Luria) in its spiritual purity, concepts that are subtle and beyond the physical level, in such a way, that would enable every beginner to approach this wisdom without falling into any kind of identification.

By understanding the Ten Luminous Emanations, an opening will be made toward understanding and knowing all the other matters in this divine wisdom.

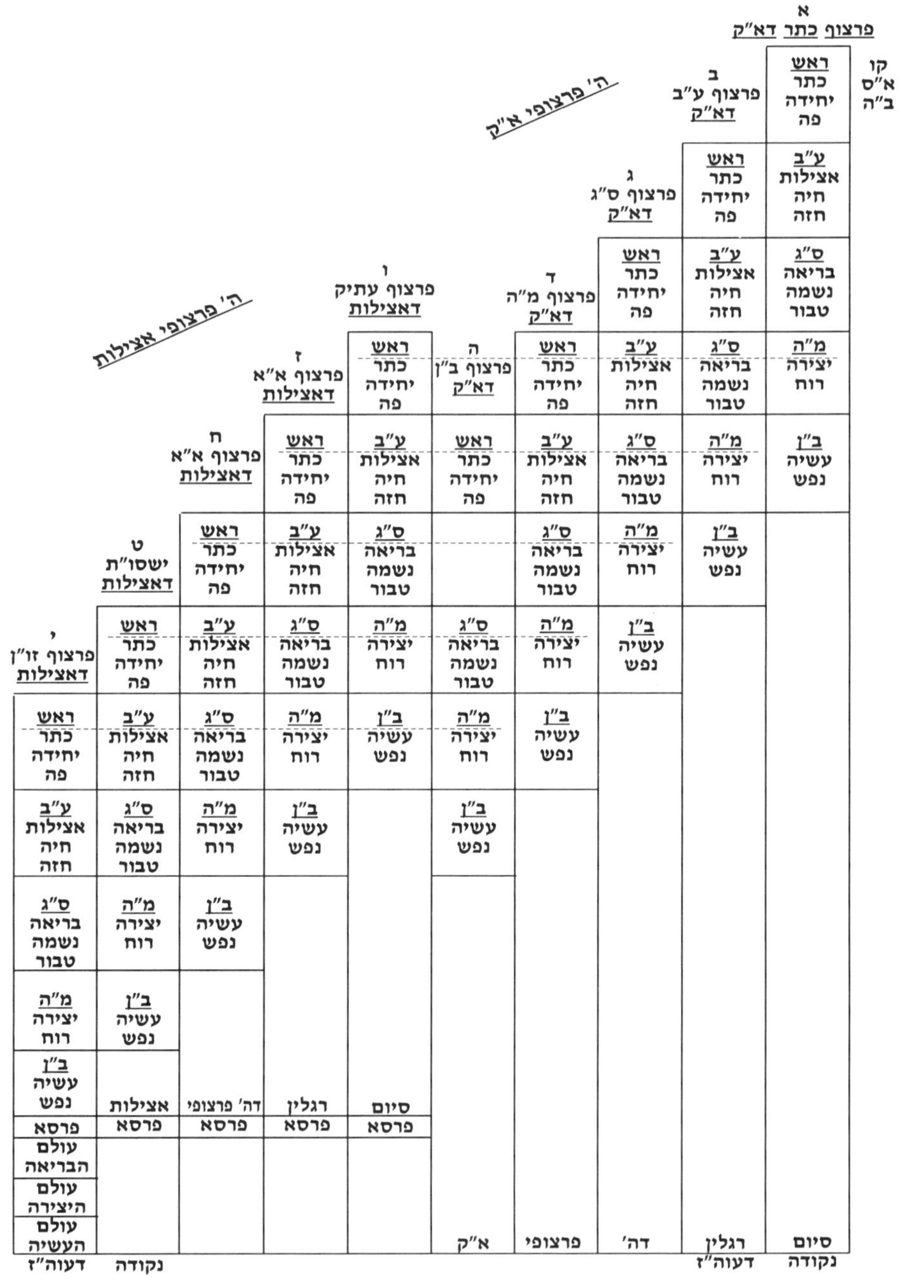

קו א"ס ב"ה

ה' פרצופי א"ק — *ה' פרצופי אצילות*

Each partzuf below is divided into five levels, read top→bottom:
`ראש / כתר / יחידה / פה` · `ע"ב / אצילות / חיה / חזה` · `ס"ג / בריאה / נשמה / טבור` · `מ"ה / יצירה / רוח` · `ב"ן / עשיה / נפש`

א — פרצוף כתר דא"ק	ב — פרצוף ע"ב דא"ק	ג — פרצוף ס"ג דא"ק	ד — פרצוף מ"ה דא"ק	ה — פרצוף ב"ן דא"ק	ו — פרצוף עתיק דאצילות	ז — פרצוף א"א דאצילות	ח — פרצוף א"א דאצילות	ט — ישסו"ת דאצילות	י — פרצוף זו"ן דאצילות
ראש כתר יחידה פה									
ע"ב אצילות חיה חזה	ראש כתר יחידה פה								
ס"ג בריאה נשמה טבור	ע"ב אצילות חיה חזה	ראש כתר יחידה פה							
מ"ה יצירה רוח	ס"ג בריאה נשמה טבור	ע"ב אצילות חיה חזה	ראש כתר יחידה פה		ראש כתר יחידה פה				
ב"ן עשיה נפש	מ"ה יצירה רוח	ס"ג בריאה נשמה טבור	ע"ב אצילות חיה חזה	ראש כתר יחידה פה	ע"ב אצילות חיה חזה	ראש כתר יחידה פה			
	ב"ן עשיה נפש	מ"ה יצירה רוח	ס"ג בריאה נשמה טבור	ע"ב אצילות חיה חזה	ס"ג בריאה נשמה טבור	ע"ב אצילות חיה חזה	ראש כתר יחידה פה		
		ב"ן עשיה נפש	מ"ה יצירה רוח	ס"ג בריאה נשמה טבור	מ"ה יצירה רוח	ס"ג בריאה נשמה טבור	ע"ב אצילות חיה חזה	ראש כתר יחידה פה	
			ב"ן עשיה נפש	מ"ה יצירה רוח	ב"ן עשיה נפש	מ"ה יצירה רוח	ס"ג בריאה נשמה טבור	ע"ב אצילות חיה חזה	ראש כתר יחידה פה
				ב"ן עשיה נפש		ב"ן עשיה נפש	מ"ה יצירה רוח	ס"ג בריאה נשמה טבור	ע"ב אצילות חיה חזה
							ב"ן עשיה נפש	מ"ה יצירה רוח	ס"ג בריאה נשמה טבור
								ב"ן עשיה נפש	מ"ה יצירה רוח
									ב"ן עשיה נפש

Lower boundary labels (left → right along the base):

אצילות | דה' פרצופי | רגלין | סיום
פרסא | פרסא | פרסא | פרסא | פרסא

עולם הבריאה
עולם היצירה
עולם העשיה

א"ק | פרצופי | דה' | רגלין | סיום

דעוה"ז — נקודה — נקודה — דעוה"ז

THE FIVE PARTZUFIM OF ADAM KADMON
AND
THE FIVE PARTZUFIM OF ATZILUTH

KNOW THAT BEFORE THE EMANATIONS WERE EMANATED AND THE CREATED WERE CREATED, THE EXALTED AND SIMPLE LIGHT HAD FILLED THE ENTIRE EXISTENCE etc. This sentence needs clarification, because before the worlds were emanated, how can there be an aspect of space and a place for any existence so that the Light had filled it completely? Also "the arousal of the desire to restrict Himself in order to reveal the perfection of His deeds" needs clarification.

Was there, God forbid, some lack in the "Endless"? And the matter of the Central Point where Restriction took place is quite surprising. For it has already been stated that there is no head (beginning) and no end, so how can there be a middle or center?

Surely, these matters are as deep as the depths of the Ocean, so I have to elaborate on them and explain them in detail.

> **There isn't anything in all existence that is not included within Endless. Our paradoxical conceptions are included within Him and are explained in the mystery of the idea that He is One, Unique, and Special.**
> אין סוף

1) Know that there is no essence of any entity in the world, those that we can conceive with our senses and those that are grasped with our minds, that are not included in the Creator. All are extended from Him. How can someone give what he doesn't possess already?

This matter is well explained in the books. Nevertheless, we should understand that all these conceptions are separate from each other, according to our minds, or even paradoxical or opposite from each other, like for example the term wisdom and sweetness. Wisdom is different from sweetness and is therefore separate from it. And also there is the difference between the doer and his deed. This can be seen very well in opposite terms like sweetness and bitterness, and so forth. Within Him, wisdom, delight, sweetness, bitterness, the doer and the deed, all are included as One in His Simple Light, without any difference between them at all. As stated in the mystery of the idea: One, Unique, and Special.

"One" shows that he is in complete unity and wholeness without any differences or opposites. "Unique" shows us what is extended from Him, even though all these multiple terms are included in Him in a Unique way like His being. And "Special" shows us that even though He is revealed in many ways, there remains only one force that motivates all of them, in such a manner, that they all return and gather into a Unique form. This uniqueness eliminates all the other forms that are revealed by his deeds. אחד, יחיד ומיוחד

The Rambam explained the idea of Wholeness which appears in the mystery of "One, Unique, and Special". He explains that the *Sefer Yetzirah* (*Book of Formation*) describes the difference between His Oneness, His Uniqueness and His Specialty. When He specializes to act in a certain way, He is called Special. And when He is divided to act each part differently, He is called Unique. And when He acts evenly, He is called One.

This means that when He specializes to act in a certain way, His action is to share His benevolence as is fit for Him — His Specialty. And there is no change or difference whatsoever in his actions. So when there is a division in His actions and differences between them, and they seem contradictory, in one action doing good while in the other doing bad, then He is called Unique. Because in every deed there is the Unique purpose of a desire to do good. Therefore we find that He is Unique in each and every action, and does not change by His different actions.

And when He acts evenly, He is called One. Which means that it reflects upon His Essence, where all opposites are even and equal within Him.

As the Rambam stated, within Him the knower, the known and the knowledge are one, for His thoughts are greatly elevated from ours, שאצלו היודע והידוע והמדע אחד הם and His ways from ours.

The two aspects of sharing before reaching the actual receiving, and after reaching actual receiving.

2) Let us learn from the eaters of the Manna. The Manna is also called the "Bread from Heaven", because it did not materialize when it got enclothed in our mundane world.

Our sages tell us that each and every person experienced a different taste from the Manna according to his delight. So there must have been opposite tastes as well, one tasted sweetness and another tasted bitterness. The Manna included in itself both opposite tastes at once, because a donor cannot give what he doesn't possess.

But on the other hand, how can the Manna have two different and opposite tastes at once?

We must learn that the Manna is devoid of both tastes, yet they are included within it in such a way that the receiver can differentiate for his own delight the taste he fancies.

By this method we can learn about all spiritual matters and substances. In itself, it is unique and simple, but it includes all the variable forms of the world. And when it reaches a receiver in the mundane and limited level of this world, then he will make a different form out of it. This form is one out of innumerable forms that are included in the spiritual substance.

That's why we should realize that there are two aspects to His benevolence: the first is the form of the essence of the spiritual abundance before it reaches the state of receiving; and the second is after the abundance has reached the state of receiving, at which time it has possessed a different and partial form according to the desire of the receiver. הנקראים נפש, רוח, נשמה, חיה, יחידה

How can we understand that the soul is a part of the divine?

3) We shall try to understand what the Kabbalists have explained about the essence of the soul. In their words, the soul is part of the divine essence of God, (the whole all-embracing Unity of existence), and there is no difference between them, except that the soul is considered to be *part* of "the whole". Like a rock that has been hewn from a mountain, the essence of the mountain and the essence of the rock are the same, there is no difference between them, except that the rock is a part of the mountain, while the mountain is considered as the "whole".

This is the main idea that is represented by our sages. And it seems to be very strange and even hard to grasp. How can the soul be different from the divine essence and part of it at the same time, and to say that it is like a rock that has been hewn from the mountain. For the rock is severed from the mountain by an axe. But how can we claim that the divine essence has been severed?

Spiritual essence is severed by dissimilarity of form as the physical world is severed by an axe.

4) Before we delve into the explanation, let us clarify the matter of difference or dissimilarity in the spiritual realm.

We should know, that spiritual people differ from each other only by dissimilarity of their spiritual form. Which means that if something spiritual changed, and became two different entities, these entities are two different forms of being. This happens in human beings and other spiritual entities.

For we already know the spiritual law about the multiple souls (*Nefesh*) that are equal to the number of bodies that these souls illuminate. Nevertheless, these souls are different in their spiritual form or essence from the bodies. That's why our sages have said that as their faces are different from each other, so their minds are different, and that the body is able to show the difference between the forms of the souls. So we can distinguish between a good soul or a bad one and other differences as well.

We can see that as physical matter is severed and becomes different by the blow of the axe, and by being far apart, so does the spiritual essence differ in form from part to part, because of the dissimilarity between them. And the more the dissimilarity, the farther apart these spiritual parts become.

How can there be dissimilarity between the creation and the Endless?

5) Nevertheless, we are still dealing with souls (*Nefesh*) of human beings who belong to the mundane world. *Nefesh* is the lowest part of soul that is connected to the body. But what about the upper part of soul (*Neshamah*), which has been previously explained to be part of the divine essence? We haven't received an explanation yet how it has been severed from the divine essence, and is now called part of it!

We cannot claim that it does not resemble the divine essence. Because it has been already explained that the divine essence is in absolute unity and Oneness. This simple Light includes all kinds of forms, and opposite forms as well in His absolute unity by the mystery of "One, Unique, and Special". So how can we even imagine dissimilarity between the soul and the divine that has caused the soul to be different from Him and have a different name? אחד, יחיד ומיוחד

Frankly, this question may be raised especially about the Light of the Endless before the Restriction. Because the reality we have before our eyes, all the worlds, upper and lower together, may be divided into two aspects. The first one is the aspect of existence before the Restriction where everything was beyond any limit and without an end. This is called the Endless Light.

The second aspect of existence is revealed from the Restriction onwards, where everything is limited and has an end. This aspect has the names of the four worlds: *Atziluth, Briah, Yetzirah,* and *Assiah.*

It is already known that we have no conception whatsoever of His essential being at all, and that He has no name or title. If we cannot grasp something in our minds, how can we give it a name?

A name always shows our ability to conceive of something. The name also shows what we conceive of it. So of course regarding His essence we have no name at all. All the names and titles that we use, are related to His Light that extends from Him.

This extension or expansion of His Light, before Restriction, filled the entire existence without any limit or end at all. This is called the "Endless". That's why the Light of the Endless has a definition, and has extended from His essence in such a manner that enables us to grant it a name, just like the name "soul". (רוח)

The clarification of the sages saying: "There has been effort and labor prepared for the reward of the souls".

6) We shall extend our mind as far as possible to understand as best we can matters dealing with such high and holy concepts.

What is the purpose of the entire existence we observe before us? Can an action be done without a purpose? If there is a purpose, which there obviously is, what is it? Why does it deserve the creation of everything in existence, including the upper and lower worlds?

Our sages have already taught us in many places, that all the worlds were created only for the nation of Israel who study the Torah and follow its precepts.

But we should fully understand why the sages have asked the question. If the purpose of the creation is to share the benevolence of the creator with his created beings, why did He have to create this mundane world? This world which is so full of misery and mishaps? Without creating it He surely could have been able to cause satisfaction and give delight to the souls as much as He wanted. So why did He have to bring the souls down into a harsh and dense body?

The reason is that in every free gift there is a slight flaw of embarrassment. In order to allow the souls to eliminate this flaw, He created this world. There is an opportunity here for the souls to labor and in the future to enjoy the reward. When they receive their reward it will be fully gained, without any feeling of embarrassment or "Bread of Shame".

The award of eternal delight for 70 years of labor is a freely given gift.

7) Our sages' words are very confusing and hard to understand. The first difficulty arises when we are told that the main purpose of our prayers is to relieve us of "Bread of Shame". Then we are told we will be receiving a great treasure freely.

Our sages inform us that this great and freely given treasure is waiting for the highest of the souls that exist in the world. This explanation only makes it more difficult to understand.

Previously, they had claimed that there is a great disadvantage in having the feeling of "Bread of Shame", in other words, the embarrassment of receiving a freely given gift. לחם בזיון

Because of that, the Creator prepared this world where there is an opportunity for spiritual labor and effort, in order to receive their reward in the world to come.

This explanation is hard to accept, it is like a person saying to his friend, please work for me for a second, and I will give you all the pleasure of this world and will bring you delight forever. This is a free gift. The reward is out of proportion to the effort. Our efforts and spiritual labor in this world which is only temporary, and quite worthless, cannot be compared with the value of the eternal delight and pleasures of the world to come. How can we even start to compare the time of a temporary world and timeless eternity?

Even more how can we compare the quality of effort with the quality of pleasure and delight that is given as a reward?

Our sages have proclaimed: "The Lord, in the future, shall bequeath 310 worlds for the righteous".

We can't say that the Creator gives part of the reward for this effort, while the other part is given as a free gift. What benefit do we receive from our sages' measurements? The "Bread of Shame" still remains as a flaw in the rest of the reward. נהמא דכסופא

We must therefore conclude that it is impossible to understand the depth of their sayings if we take them according to their face value. We should try to grasp the deep meaning that is hidden behind these words.

The entire existence was emanated and created by a single thought. This thought is the activator, the essence of the action, reward, and spiritual effort. And this is the essence of the reward that is sought and also the essence of the spiritual effort.

8) Before we start clarifying our sages' words, we should understand the Thought of Creation. The creation of the worlds and the existence we know was not done by many thoughts, as is our own way. He is One, Unique, and Special, as previously stated. And as He is Simple, so are His Lights that He illuminates. They are Simple, and do not possess many different forms, as is stated in the verse: "My thoughts are not like your thoughts, and my ways are not like your ways, etc.".
כי לא מחשבותי כמחשבותיכם וכו'

So we should understand that all the names and titles, and all the upper and lower worlds are included in the All Embracing Unity of His Simple Light. And within Him, the Light, the Thought, the Action, the Doer and all that our minds can think of are One.

Accordingly, we are able to see that in one Thought the entire existence was emanated and created, including the upper and lower worlds, until the end of the Tikune. And this sole thought is the activator of all deeds, the essence of each and every action, the essence of the spiritual effort, the recipient of the reward and is itself the essence of the existing reward that is sought when complete perfection is reached, as explained by our great Kabbalist, the Ramban.

The Restriction explains how it can be that from a perfect action, imperfection came to be!

9) The Ari explained at length, in the first chapters of this book, about the Restriction (*Tzimtzum*). It is one of the most serious subjects of Kabbalah. צמצום

We may come to the conclusion that all the corruption

and all perversion come directly from Him (God forbid!) As is stated in the verse "He forms (produces) bad and creates good". יוצר אור ובורא חושך

How can that be? How can all the bad come from Him? It is completely opposite to His essential being. And how can it reside in the Light that is full of pleasure and delight only?

We can't say that there are two different thoughts that oppose each other in Him.

So how can it be that all this comes from Him, and extends down to this world, which is full of misery, impurity and even great filth. And how do they reside together in one simple Thought?

THE THOUGHT OF CREATION

10) We have reached a stage where we have to clarify the Thought of Creation. As has been said nothing is done without previous thought. Even in a human being who has many thoughts in his mind, the eventual deed was at first a thought. For example, when a person builds his home, we assume that he thought of the image of the house and then proceeded with the other thoughts and deeds necessary to accomplish the first thought of the image of the house.

So we can see that the end of the deed was already in the first thought, including the completeness of it which is to impart pleasure and delight to all the created beings, as explained in the Zohar (the *Book of Splendor*).

It is known that His Thought is completed immediately, because He is not a human being, and does not need action to fulfill His Thought.

By this it can be understood, that when He had the thought of creation, immediately the Light was revealed and drawn down from Him, in all Its full and complete appearance with the utmost revelation of pleasure and delight.

All of this was included in the one and same thought that is called the "Thought of Creation". And you should know that this thought of creation is also called the "Endless Light" because we have no word or name to define His divine essential Being.

From the force of the desire to share of the Emanator, the desire to receive was born inevitably in the emanated. This is the vessel in

which the emanated receives the abundance.

11) This is what the Ari referred to by saying that at first the Endless Light filled all existence. Meaning that as soon as He thought to impart pleasure upon the created beings, and the Light expanded from Him, the desire to receive His abundance was immediately impressed in His Light.

We can also say that this desire is equal to the entire expanding Light. In other words, the quantity of the Light and His abundance, is equal to the desire to receive it, not more nor less!

So the essence of this desire to receive that is impressed in the Light, is called place or room. For example, we can say that a person has a place or room to accept a certain amount of food, while the other person has only half or less room. מקום

With what sort of place or room are we dealing? Not in the size of the stomach, but in the "size" of the desire and the nature of the longing to receive the food.

So you can see that the size of the room or place to receive the food depends on the degree and nature of the desire to eat. Moreover in spirituality, the desire to receive the abundance is the place for it. And the quantity is determined by how much room there is, or how strong the desire to receive it is. רצון לקבל

The desire to receive that is included in the Thought of Creation, has caused His essential being to be revealed by the word "Endless".

12) I shall further clarify how the Light of the Endless

departed from His essential being which has no word or utterance, and received a defined name, the Endless Light.

The reason for this lies in the fact that there is a distinction in the Light, between the desire to receive that is impressed in Him and the divine Essence. This desire is a new aspect that is not included at all in His divine Essence because it is impossible for Him to receive from anyone or anything.

And this new form of desire, is the entire being of this Light. Please try to understand the depth of this matter because it is impossible to delve into it any further!

Before the Restriction the difference of form in the desire to receive was indistinguishable.

13) In His Almightiness, the new form was not detected, and there was no dissimilarity between it and His Light.

This is the explanation of the mystery that appears in the "Chapters of Rabbi Eliezer", that before the world was created, there was a state of being, described in the verse "He is One and His Name is One". "He" refers to the Light of the Endless, and "His Name" refers to the place or the mystery of the desire to receive from His divine Essence, which is included in the "Light of the Endless".

Furthermore, "He is One and His Name is One", meaning "His Name" is the secret of *Malkhut* of the Endless, which is the mystery of desire. In other words, the desire to receive that is impressed upon the entire existence that is included in the Thought of Creation, before the Restriction, had no difference of form or dissimilarity with the Light in it. The Light and the place are one. Because if there were any difference or any lack in that place in relation to the Light of the Endless, there would definitely have been two different aspects. הוא אחד ושמו אחד

Restriction means that the Malkhut of the Endless reduced its desire to receive, then the Light disappeared. Because there can be no Light if there is no vessel.

14) This is the matter of Restriction, where the desire to receive that is included in the Light of the Endless, named the *Malkhut* of the Endless, which is the Mystery of the Thought of Creation in the "Endless", that includes the entire existence, adorned itself by rising in itself to be equal in its form as much as possible to the Divine Essence. מלכות אין־סוף

It reduced its desire to receive in its fourth phase from receiving the great abundance from Him so that all the worlds would be emanated and created until this world is reached. In that manner, the desire to receive would be completed and would return to its aspect of sharing. And that's how it came to be equal in its form to the Emanator and resemble Him.

After it had reduced the desire to receive, the Light had disappeared from there, because it is already known that the Light depends on the desire. And the desire is the place for the Light to be revealed, because there is no compulsion in spirituality.

THE CRAVING OF THE SOUL

15) And now we shall clarify how the soul is carved from the Endless. It has already been said that the soul is a part of the upper Divine Essence. And formerly we asked, how and by what means can the form of the soul be different from His simple Light in such a manner that it becomes completely separated from the All Embracing Unity?

It is now understood that there truly has been a great difference of form in the soul. For even though there is included in Him all the forms and images that we can possibly think of, after what has been already explained, you can find one form that is not included in Him, this is the desire to receive. For there is no one for Him to receive from!

However the main purpose for creating the souls was to impart upon them pleasure and delight, which is also the Thought of Creation. So inevitably, this law was impressed in the souls, meaning, the desire to receive His abundance and to long for it.

This is how the souls differ from Him. Their spiritual form is different from Him now. Formerly we explained that physical matter is separated by distance and motion, while spiritual essence is separated and becomes different from each other by the difference of their spiritual form.

The measure of distance between souls is the extent of the dissimilarity. So that if the difference of form reaches a complete oppositeness, then there is a complete separation and severance. They become complete strangers to each other and are not able to draw anything from each other!

**After the Restriction and the veil
was made to conceal the desire to
receive, it is not appropriate anymore to be a ves-sel for receiving.
And it has separated from the holy
system of the creation (Kedusha).
Instead the Returning Light is being
used as a vessel, while the desire to
receive has been given to the unholy
system of the creation (Tum'ah).**

16) After the Restriction and the veil that was made to
cover this vessel that is called the desire to receive, it ceased to
exist and was separated from the holy system of creation. Instead
the Returning Light was installed to be the vessel of recipiency.

You should know that this is the entire and only difference between the four worlds — *Atziluth, Briah, Yetzirah,* and
Assiah (action) — of the holy system and the four worlds of the
unholy system. Because the vessel of recipiency of the four worlds
of holiness originates from the Returning Light, which is repaired
(*Tikune*) to be in conformity with the Endless Light. On the
other hand, the four worlds of unholiness use the desire to receive
for itself and is in complete difference of form from the
"Endless". That is why it is cut off completely from the true origin of the Light force — the Endless Light. תיקון

**The human being feeds on what the
unholy system (Klippot) produces.
That's why he uses the desire to
receive like it.**

17) That's how we can understand the source of corruption and the spoil that was included immediately in the

Thought of Creation, which is to impart pleasure and delight upon the created.

After all the five worlds were evolved, including: *Adam Kadmon, Atziluth, Briah, Yetzirah* and *Assiah* (Action), the five worlds of unholiness were also revealed, by the mystery of the verse: "We are then affronted by this foul body", which is related to the verse: "the desire of his heart is evil from his youth." Because all his nourishment from when he's young is from the productions of the unholy system. All that the *Klippot* or the unholiness cares for is based on the "desire to receive for oneself alone" and they have no desire to share whatsoever. א"ק ואבי"ע

The entire existence that is included in the Endless is extended from an existence that already exists. And only the desire to receive is new. All is drawn from a non-existing state.

18) You should know that the entire matter of the new existence that the Creator brought forward in this creation, which is also explained by our sages as being created from a non-existing state, is related only to the desire to receive pleasure that is impressed in every created being. Even more so, nothing has been newly created by the creation.

The verse "He formed light and created darkness" is explained by the Ramban: the word "created" refers to a new appearance of something that was not there before. As you can see, it does not say "He created light", which means that there was no new appearance, e.g., by revealing something that did not exist before. The Light and all that is included in It, is all the Light that is conceived and grasped in the world. All this is extended from what already exists. That means that it is included already in Him. So there is no new appearance. יוצר אור ובורא חושך

That's why it is said that "He formed the light", meaning that it is not new or created. The darkness includes all the displeasing things in the world. It has been said, "He created darkness", because it appeared from a non-existing state. בורא חושך

In other words, there is no darkness in Him, it newly appeared. And the source of it all is the desire to receive the pleasure that is included in the Light that extends from Him, and is from the beginning denser than the Exalted Light, so it is called darkness compared to the Light. But eventually, the *Klippot* (husks) or unholy system appears and the wicked, who are completely severed from the source of life, appear. קליפות

This is the secret of the verse: "Her legs are drawn downwards to death". The word "legs" means "end". "Her legs" refers to *Malkhut* (Kingdom), which is the aspect of the desire to receive pleasure that exists in the extension of the Light and in the end, death, to the unholy system and to all those who are connected to it and feed on it. מלכות

As we are considered to be branches of the "Endless", what is related to our source gives us pleasure, and what is not, causes us misery and discomfort.

19) We may ask whether the difference of form caused by the desire to receive has to be in the created beings. If not, how can they extend from Him and become created beings, for this cannot be unless there is a difference of form caused by the desire to receive pleasure. Moreover, this desire is the main

essence of the creation and the Thought of Creation is based upon it. It is also the level and quantity of pleasure and delight as explained previously. That is why it is called space. So how can it possibly be called darkness (God forbid), and be extended until it reaches the aspect of death as it severs the receivers from the source of life? And we should further understand what is the great anxiety and anger that is aroused in the receivers below because of the difference of form from the Creator?

In order to understand this matter we should explain what is the source of pleasure and misery that are felt in our world.

As we know, the nature of every branch is equal to its root or source. So everything that appears in the root should please the branch, while all that which doesn't appear in the root shouldn't. On the contrary, the branch would dislike it. This law appears in every relationship of root and branch.

Just as He is the root and Source of all His created beings, so all that is included in Him and is drawn to us from Him directly, causes us immediate delight because our nature is close to our source and resembles it. While all that does not appear in Him, and are not drawn to us directly from Him but from the opposite side of the creation, is against our nature and we cannot abide it.

In other words, we like to be at rest, and we hate to be in motion. So the purpose of every movement we are involved in is to reach a state of rest and security. This is because our source is motionless and in complete rest.

That's why we adore wisdom, courage, gallantry, riches and all the good qualities that are also included in Him, our

Source. And we hate all that is opposite these qualities, such as ignorance, weakness, poverty, etc. They do not exist in our Source at all, that's why we dislike them.

Nevertheless we should ask, how can we receive something that doesn't come directly from Him but from the hatred of created beings. This is like the story of a rich man who invites a poor man from the street, and feeds him, offers him drink, and gives him silver and gold. And every day he offers him more and more.

The poor man feels two kinds of feeling from the great amount of gifts that he is receiving. On one hand, he is feeling the greatest pleasure and infinite delight from the gifts, while on the other hand, it is hard for him to bear this abundance and is ashamed to receive it.

Of course, the pleasure he gets from the gifts comes directly from the wealthy man, while the embarrassment that he feels comes from the nature of the recipient himself.

A feeling of shame is aroused in him because of receiving a free gift. But in an indirect way, it is also caused by the rich man.

We are ashamed of our desire to receive because it does not exist in our Source. This is according to our sages' "sayings". In order to eliminate this feeling He has "prepared" for us in this world spiritual labor in Torah and precepts to transform our desire to receive to a desire to share.

20) What we can conclude from all that has been said until now is that all that is drawn down to us other than from Him causes us a feeling of shame and discomfort, and is against our nature.

And the new form that appears in the recipient, the desire to receive pleasure, is not a flaw in Him. On the contrary, it is the main purpose of His creation. And without it there would be no revelation of the Creator at all.

But the recipient, who has this desire, feels discomfort because his own nature is different from his Source.

We have been able till now to understand the saying of our sages that this world was created to overcome this feeling of shame.

He created this world to enable the soul to come into a body. And by studying the Torah and doing the precepts for the sake of the Creator, the vessels of the desire to receive of the soul are transformed to vessels of sharing. In other words, from the soul's point of view it is not interested in receiving any abundance. It is ready to receive it only for the pleasure of the Creator.

Consequently, the soul is clear of the desire to receive for oneself alone, it does not feel any "bread of shame", and is able to fulfill the purpose of the creation.

The necessity of creating this world that is so far from the "Endless" will be further explained, as the spiritual labor of transforming the desire to receive to the desire to share cannot be done except in this world.

The loss of the wicked is doubled while the inheritance of the righteous shall be multiplied.

21) The loss of the wicked is doubled, because they try to hold on to the rope from both sides. As this world is created

with lack and emptiness, without all the abundance, and in order to achieve all the necessities we need to be in motion all the time. And it is known that continuous motion causes sorrow and anguish, because it doesn't exist in the essence of the Creator. On the other hand, it is impossible to be motionless if the created beings are to fulfill their needs, and this also is contrary to the nature of their Source, Who is full of pleasure and delight.

So they choose the misery of being in continuous motion in order to fulfill their needs. But because all their achievements are for themselves alone, and they want to double their possessions all the time, they die without even fulfilling half of their desires.

That's how they suffer from both sides, from the side of continuous motion and also from the side of their possessions, because they hardly ever complete them.

While the righteous after they have transformed their desire to receive to the desire to share and all that they receive is for the sake of sharing, their inheritance is multiplied. Because, not only do they receive the full pleasure and delight from all their possessions, they also achieve complete unity with the Light. And then they are restful and have peace of mind because all that they get comes by itself without any motion or labor.

The Thought of Creation compels all the details of existence to correlate with each other until the end of the Tikune process.

22)   And now, after achieving all this, we can begin to understand the greatness of His Unity, about which it has been said "His Thoughts are different from our thoughts". All the multiple matters and different forms that we can conceive of in the entire existence, are all included in one single thought — the Thought of Creation.

This thought, which is also the thought to bring pleasure and delight to all beings, encompasses all the existence and brings it to a unified whole until the end of the Tikune process. It is the sole purpose of creation. His thought is the activator. In other words, by the power of the activator in the action everything is simultaneously activated. What is considered to be in Him only a thought, is a law among His beings. So because He has thought to give us pleasure, our actions are activated by this power, and it is also the action itself.

So, as the desire to receive pleasure has already been impressed upon us, we may consider ourselves to be the "action". The difference of form between us and Him, is that we are created beings and therefore different from Him. That means the Activator has revealed His action.

This action is also considered to be the labor, caused by the power of the Activator in His action, which increases the desire and the amount of pleasure in us. And by this power all the worlds are developed and connected to each other until the aspect of complete separation of the body and our world is reached, with complete severance from the source of life.

This separation is caused by the utter impossibility to share anything at all beyond its boundaries, which in turn, brings death upon the bodies and all kinds of misery to the soul.

This is the matter of spiritual labor in the Torah and its precepts. Because by illuminating the Line in the place that has been restricted, the holy names of the Torah and its precepts are drawn in. And by laboring in the Torah and its precepts for the sake of the Creator thereby bestowing satisfaction upon Him, the vessels of the desire to receive in us are gradually transformed to the desire to share. And this is all the reward that is sought and hopefully may be received by us.

As long as our desire to receive is not ready yet, we are not able to open up and receive his great abundance. All this is caused by the fear of difference of form from him, which was the reason for the Tzimtzum (Restriction). By preparing our vessel for the sake of sharing, we resemble our Creator and are fit to receive all the pleasure and delight infinitely. צמצום

So you can see that all the multiple and opposite forms of the creation we see, which includes the forms of activator and activated, damage and repair, labor and rewards, etc. are all included in one single Thought of the Creator, for the purpose of bestowing pleasure and delight, not more nor less.

Similarly, many different kinds of understandings and beliefs are included, belief in our holy Torah, and even other beliefs as well, the many created beings and worlds and the different ways of each of them, all these are derived from the one and only Thought as I shall explain.

The Malkhut of the Endless means that the Malkhut does not have an aspect of end. תיקוני זהר

23) By what we shall further explain, we will clarify what appears in *Tikunei Zohar* about the *Malkhut* of the Endless. For the great question is how is it that we give the name *Malkhut* in the Endless, since this would mean that there are also nine other *Sfirot* in the Endless. ספירות

From what we have previously said, the aspect of desire to receive in the Endless has been well clarified. It is also called the *Malkhut* of the Endless, the only difference being that it has no end and does not limit the Endless Light whatsoever, because the aspect of difference of form between it and the Light has not appeared yet. That's why it is called Endless — without end. While from the *Tzimtzum* onwards, an end appeared in every *Sfirah* and vessel, because of the *Malkhut.* מלכות

It is impossible for the desire to receive to appear in any vessel with-out 'the four aspects. This is the secret of the Tetragrammaton — the holy name with the four letters.

24) Let's clarify this matter, in order to understand the aspect of end that occurred in *Malkhut* and appeared because of it. מלכות

First we should understand what the Kabbalists have defined for us and is also found in the Zohar and the Tikunei Zohar; there is no Light, great or small, in the upper worlds or in the lower ones that does not allow the order of the holy name.

This also applies to the law that appears in the Tree of Life; there is no Light that appears in the worlds that is not enclothed in a vessel. In other words, I explained the difference between His Essential Being and the Light that extends from Him because of the desire to receive pleasure which is included in the Light and causes it to be differ-ent from His Essential Being which is devoid of that desire of course.

That is why this Light is defined as an Emanated Being. Because of the difference of form between It and the Creator, It became separated from the Emanator.

And it has already been explained that the desire to receive that is included in His Light is also the amount of Light as well, and is also called the place for the Light. In other words, it receives the abundance from Him according to his desire to receive, not more nor less.

And also the desire to receive is a new aspect altogether, which came with the creation of the worlds by the creation of something from non-existence. This aspect and form is not included in His Essential Being. The Creator created it only for the purpose of the creation. This is the secret of creating darkness, because this aspect is the source of darkness by its difference of form and dissimilarity from the Light. It is thicker and denser from the Light that is drawn by it and into it.

That is how every Light that extends from Him is immediately divided into two different aspects: the first one is the Essential Light that is drawn before the desire to receive pleasure is revealed and aroused in it. The second aspect is the arousal of the desire to receive this pleasure. Then the Light becomes denser and a bit darker because of reaching this difference of form.

The first aspect is the Light, while the second is the vessel. Therefore, in every extending Light there are four aspects, from the vessels point of view, in achieving this Light. Because the desire to receive, which is called the vessel in relation to the extending Light, is not completed at once. It is completed on the basis of actor and action.

And there are two aspects to the actor and two aspects to the action. They are called the power of the actor and the actor himself, and the power of the action and the action itself. Altogether there are four aspects.

The desire to receive is not completed in the emanated being, not until it is aroused from itself.

25) This is because the vessel is the source of darkness, and is opposite from the Light, so it must be aroused gradually

by cause and effect. The darkness is an offspring of the Light and is related to it, just like pregnancy and birth, which is the essence of the potential and revealed state. In other words, the aspect of desire to receive is inevitably and immediately included in the extending Light, but there is no difference of form at first, and until this desire has itself been completed "on its own", it is not yet sufficient because this desire to receive is still from the Emanator Himself. The emanated being has to reveal this desire to receive by himself. יש מאין

So the emanated has to draw the Light by his own desire to receive, more than the Light that the Emanator is extending toward him. And only when the emanated being acts on his own initiative, to enlarge his own desire, is the desire to receive completed and the Light is able to enter this vessel and stay there permanently.

But truly, the Endless Light extends, so to speak, in four aspects as well, until it reaches the completion of the desire to receive from the emanated being himself, which is the fourth aspect. There is no other way for the Light to be extended and drawn from the Creator, and to be called the "Endless". אין סוף

Nevertheless, there was no change whatsoever in His Essential Being, because of the desire to receive. And there is no difference between the Light and the place of the Light — the desire to receive pleasure. So they are one.

This is what is stated in the "Chapters of Rabbi Eliezer" that before the world was created "He is One and His Name is One". הוא אחד ושמו אחד

The question is what is the difference between Him and His Name? What is the meaning of His Name? It should have been that before the world was created He was One.

But the meaning is for the Endless Light, before the Restriction. Because even though there is place there and a desire to receive the abundance from His Essential Being, nevertheless there is no difference whatsoever between the Light and the place. So, He is One, meaning the Light of the Endless, and His Name is One, meaning the desire to receive which is included there without any difference of form at all.

Also, this is the explanation of the sages' hint that the numerical value (*gematria*) of "His Name" (*Shmo*) equals the numerical value of the word "desire" (*Ratzon*) or desire to receive pleasure. רצון

All the worlds that are included in the Thought of Creation is called the "Endless Light". And the all-inclusive recipient is called "Malkhut of the Endless".

26) We have already discussed the matter of the relation between thought and action — that there must be a previous thought to every action. By that we refer to the Thought of Creation that extended from His Essential Being to bestow pleasure and delight upon His created beings. And that the Thought and the Light are one.

So we can understand that the Endless Light that extends from Him includes the entire existence we see before us, until the end of the *Tikune* process. This is the completion of the action, while in His Thought all the created beings are fully completed in all the glory and satisfaction that He wanted to bestow.

So the entire existence is called the Endless Light and the all-inclusive recipient is called the "Endless *Malkhut*".

Even though only the fourth aspect restricted itself, the Light withdrew from all other three aspects as well.

27) It has already been made clear that the Central Point, which is the secret of the all-inclusive point of the Thought of Creation, and is also the desire to enjoy (receive); adorned itself in order to resemble the Emanator even more, although from the Emanator's side there is no difference of form whatsoever. Nevertheless the Point of the Desire felt in this is an indirect drawing from Him, as we explained by the example of the rich man and the poor man. That is why it decreased its desire from the last aspect which is the greatest desire to receive pleasure, in order to reach a greater unity with the Light that is withdrawn directly from Him.

So the aspect of place in the Light became empty; in other words, all four phases that exist in the place, even though it decreased only the fourth phase of desire. Because there is no division into separate parts in the spiritual realm.

Then it returned and drew a Line of Light to the first three aspects while the fourth one stayed as an empty space.

28) After that, the Endless Light was drawn again into the place that had been emptied. But it did not fill the four phases of the place (Desire to Receive), only the first three, as this was the desire of the Central Point at the Tzimtzum. רצון לקבל

So the Central Point that restricted itself remained empty and void, because the Light enlightened only the first three phases and not the fourth.

We shall explain later on how each and every aspect of the spiritual world includes all the other aspects as well. And with this, you will understand that the four phases are included in each other. So in the fourth phase itself there are all the four phases. Consequently even in the fourth phase the Light reached the first three phases, and only the last phase remained empty without the Light. And remember this.

Wisdom is called Light, and Mercy is called water. Binah is called upper water, and Malkhut is called lower water.

29) And now we shall discuss the essence of the four aspects of cause and effect that must be accomplished in order to complete the form of the desire to receive.

In *Atziluth*, there are two aspects of Light. The first one is called Light, which is also called Wisdom. The second is water, which is also called Mercy. The first aspect is drawn from above downwards without any help from the lower beings. And the second aspect is drawn by the help of the lower beings, so it is called water. Because the nature of the Light is to be above, while the nature of water is to be below. אצילות

Also in the water there are two aspects, the upper water that is revealed by the second phase of the four phases of the vessel, and the lower water, revealed by the fourth phase itself.

The extension of the Endless Light to the four phases in order to reveal the vessel, which is the desire to receive.

30) Therefore there are ten *Sfirot* in every expansion of the Endless Light, the Endless which is considered to be the source and the Emanator, is called *Keter* (Crown). The extending Light itself is called Wisdom, which is the entire extension of the Light from above, from the Endless, Blessed be He.

And it is already known, that in every extension of the Light, the desire to receive is already included within. Except that the desire is not actually revealed until it is aroused by the emanated being himself, to desire and draw down the Light more than has already been extended.

Because the desire to receive is immediately included potentially in the Light, the Light has to reveal it. So the Light is aroused to draw an additional abundance, more than has already been extended, from the Endless. And that's how the desire to receive is actually revealed in that Light and the new aspect of difference of form is activated. Because it has become denser than the Light. This part that has become dense is called *Binah*. בינה

Actually, *Binah* is part of Wisdom, in other words the essence of the extension of the Endless Light. But because of the arousal of the desire, it drew upon itself more abundance than the amount that was extended from the Endless and caused the difference of form. It became a bit denser from the light and got a name on its own, which is *Sfirat Binah*. ספירת בינה

The essence of the additional abundance that it drew from the Endless, by the power of its own desire is called the Light of Mercy or "upper water". Because the Light is not drawn directly from the Endless as the Light of Wisdom is, but rather by the help of the emanated, it has a name of its own.

So you can see now that *Binah* includes three aspects of Lights. The first one is the essential Light of *Binah* which is part of the Light of Wisdom. The second is the aspect of density and difference of form that it achieved because of the arousal of the desire. And the third is the Light of Mercy that it receives by its own drawing of the Light from the Endless.

Nevertheless, the vessel of recipiency has not yet been completed, because *Binah* is still a part of the essence of the Light of Wisdom which is very exalted. It is a direct extension from the Light of the Endless. Only the beginning or the root of the vessel of recipiency is revealed in *Binah*, or the activator of the vessel, because after that this same Light of Mercy that has been drawn by the arousal of desire to receive, is extended again from *Binah* and the Light of Wisdom is added to it. This extension of the Light of Mercy is called *Zeir Anpin* (Small Face), or the three *Sfirot Hesed, Gevurah*, and *Tiferet.* זעיר אנפין

In this extending Light, the desire is aroused to draw a new abundance, more than the extension of the Light of Wisdom that exists in *Binah*. So this extension has also two aspects, the extending Light is called *Zeir Anpin* and the arousal of the desire is called *Malkhut.* מלכות

This is the mystery of the Ten *Sfirot. Keter* is the Endless, Wisdom is the extending Light from the Endless, *Binah* is the Light of Wisdom that was aroused to draw more abundance (that's how it became denser than the Light). *Zeir Anpin* which includes: *Hesed, Gevurah, Tiferet, Netzah, Hod, Yesod*, is the mystery of the Light of Mercy with an enlightenment of Light of Wisdom that is drawn from *Binah*; and *Malkhut* is the mystery of the second arousal for the additional Light of Wisdom (more than what is in *Zeir Anpin*). חג"ת נה"י

The four phases of desire is the secret of the Tetragrammaton. They are: Keter, hochma, Binah, Tiferet, and Malkhut.

31) This is the secret of the Tetragrammaton, *Yud-Hei-Vav-Hei*. The upper point of the Hebrew letter *Yud* is the secret of the Endless, or the potential power of the actor that is

included in the Endless: "to bestow pleasure and delight upon His created beings" which is the *Sfirah* of *Keter.* יהו"ה

The letter *Yud* is the secret of *Hochma*, the first phase, which is the aspect of potential power of the actor that is included in the extension of the Endless.

The first letter *Hei* is the secret of *Binah*, the second phase which is the aspect of revelation of the potential power, or in other words, the Light that has become denser than what it was in *Hochma*. חכמה

The letter *Vav* is the secret of *Zeir Anpin*, the extension of the Light of Mercy, that is drawn from *Binah*. It is the third phase, the potential power of the action. זעיר אנפין

The second letter *Hei* of the Tetragrammaton is the secret of *Malkhut*, the fourth phase, the revelation of the completion of the vessel from the potential state, that is also aroused to draw more than the extension of the Light from *Binah*. By this the form of desire to receive is fixed completely. And the Light is revealed in Its vessel, that is completed only in the fourth phase and not before. מלכות

By now you can understand that there is no Light in the upper or lower worlds that is not arranged according to the four letters of the Tetragrammaton which is the secret of the four phases. Because without it the desire to receive is not fixed and cannot be revealed completely. This desire has to exist in every Light, because it is both the amount of Light and also the place where it is revealed.

The letters Yud (י) and Vav (ו) are

thin because they are in a potential state only.

32) The letter *Yud* is related to *Hochma*, and the letter *Hei* to *Binah*, and the entire essence of the Light that exists in the ten *Sfirot* exists entirely in *Hochma*, while *Binah, Zeir Anpin* and *Malkhut* are considered to be only clothing compared to *Hochma*. The question that may arise is: then shouldn't *Hochma* have been expressed by the biggest letter of the Tetragrammaton? ספירות

But the essence of the matter is that the letters of the Tetragrammaton do not express the amount of Light of the ten *Sfirot*. They only express how the vessel experiences the revelation of the Light. The white part of the parchment of the Torah scroll is related to the aspect of the Light. And the black part is the letters of the Torah scroll that is related to the aspect of the vessels. ספירות

Therefore the *Keter*, since it is only in the aspect of "the potential state", or the root of the root of the vessel, it appears only as the upper point of the letter *Yud*. And *Hochma*, in the aspect of the potential power before it becomes revealed, is expressed by the small letter *Yud*, which is the smallest letter of them all. *Binah*, where the potential power is revealed, is expressed by the longer letter *Hei*. And *Zeir Anpin*, because it is only the potential state of action, is expressed by the long and thin letter *Vav*. The thin shape indicates that the vessel exists in it but is still in a potential state and is not revealed yet, because the extension of *Hochma* is not sufficient to reveal a complete vessel. *Binah* also is not a complete one but only the aspect of an actor of a vessel. So the "leg" of the Hebrew letter *Yud* is short, indicating that it did not reveal by its power and extension an aspect of a complete vessel.

Malkhut also is expressed by the letter *Hei* just as *Binah* is. It is revealed by a fully formed and large letter. Now, both are expressed by the same letter, because in the world of *Tikune* they are really the same and resemble each other and borrow their vessels from each other as well, as is said in the verse "They both go together."

Spiritual motion means renewing the difference of form.

33) The subject of time and motion still has to be clarified, as we deal with them continuously in the wisdom of Kabbalah.

As you know, spiritual movement does not resemble movement according to our senses, from place to place. The intention is to refer to a difference of form. So every change and new appearance is called motion.

This change, or difference of form, that has newly appeared in the spiritual realm, and is different from its former being, is considered to be separated from it and becomes further apart. It becomes fully in control on its own behalf.

This makes it look like a physical essence that a part has been severed from it. This part moves and can go from place to place on its own. So the appearance of the new form is called motion.

Spiritual time means a number of new appearances, that relate subordinately, by cause and effect, before and after.

34) Time in its spiritual definition is different from what we perceive by our senses. Time according to us is a sequence of feelings of motion. In our minds we imagine, by drawing a pattern of a number of actions, that we feel one after the other and copy them into an imaginary "time" zone. Thus, if a person and his surroundings were in complete rest, he wouldn't know anything about time.

So it is in the spiritual realm, the total amount of new appearances in their difference of form that are considered to be in spiritual motion, and are related to each other by cause and effect, is called "time", spiritually. And the idea of before and after always means cause and effect.

All the substance that is related to the emanated being consists of the desire to receive. And all that is beyond that relates to the Emanator.

35) Bear in mind, that the aspect of the desire to receive in the emanated, that has been thoroughly clarified, is his vessel. And you should know that it is the general and entire substance that is related to the emanated, in such a manner that all existence besides it belongs to the Emanator.

The desire to receive is the first and basic form of every essential being, and this form is called substance or matter, because we have no perception in essence.

36) Even though the aspect of "desire to receive" is seemingly understood as the form and revelation of essence, how can we grasp it as the substance of the essence? רצון לקבל

This is the case with all essence in our immediate surroundings. Our custom is to call the first or basic form as the basic substance of the essence, because we cannot grasp matter at all. Our five senses are not equipped for that. These senses: seeing, hearing, smelling, tasting and feeling, provide our intellectual mind with only abstract forms of changing essence, that are drawn into our minds and then organized through our five senses.

For example, if we take the microscopic atom, which is the basic element of matter, and reduce it further, there remains only abstract forms that are perceived. Or to be more exact they are perceived through our "desire to receive and to be received" that we find in them. And by this law of actions and reactions we are able to perceive them and distinguish between the various kinds, until we reach the basic substance of this essence. And even then they are only the potential power of force of the essence and not matter itself.

So you can see for yourself, that even in our mundane world we have no other way to conceive matter except if we base our assumption on the fact that the basic form is matter that includes within itself all the changes, forms, and events. And of course, this is the same with the upper worlds that are beyond our senses and imagination .

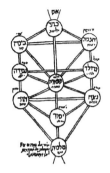

APPENDICES

Kabbalistic Terminology Volume One
A Schedule of Questions and Answers
Biographical Sketches
Rabbi Isaac Luria
Rabbi Yehuda Ashlag

THE UPPER TRIANGLE

כתר
KETER

בינה
BINAH

וחכמה
HOKHMAH

THE SEVEN SFIROT

Seven forms and levels of cosmic intelligence - the manifestation of the Lightforce

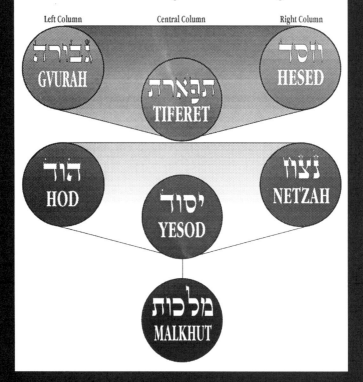

Left Column   Central Column   Right Column

גבורה
GVURAH

חסד
HESED

תפארת
TIFERET

הוד
HOD

נצח
NETZAH

יסוד
YESOD

מלכות
MALKHUT

These intelligence-coded messages (metaphysical DNA) account for our grand solar system and for the earth's cosmic division. The seven Sfirot are encased in the heart and soul of the planets. The shell of each planet is an aspect of body consciousness.

KABBALISTIC TERMINOLOGY

1) Light - (מהו אור) Al and any essence (received or existing) in the worlds as existence emerging from existence. For this includes and comprises all existence except the substance that pertains and relates to the substance of the vessels.

2) Light and Vessel - (מהם אור וכלי) The desire to receive of the emanated being is called vessel. The beneficence or bestowal it receives is called light.

3) Circular Light - (מהו אור עגול) This is the light which does not make or cause distinction.

4) Simple Light - (מהו אור פשוט) This is the state of light which includes within it the vessel without any distinctions between the light and the vessel.

5) Light of Wisdom - (מהו אור החכמה) The light which is drawn to the emanated being in the first extension which comprises the essence and life of the emanated being.

6) Light of Mercy - (מהו אור דחסדים) A concept of light (energy) which enclothes (and thus reveals) the light of Wisdom and is drawn to the emanated being with the first extension.

7) Empty Atmosphere -(מהו אויר ריקני) Light (energy) of Mercy before it enclothes the Light of Wisdom.

8) Afterwards - (מהו אחר־כך) A resultant phase proceeding from the preceding one.

9) Middle - (מהו אמצעית) See # 39

10) One - (מהו אחד) The upper Light which is extended as His essence in a state of complete and simple unity, and just as It exists in the Endless, so It exists in the World of Action, without any change or addition. Therefore it is called One.

11) Creator - (מהו בורא) The name Creator is uniformly applied to any new revelation which manifests as existence from non -existence which is the substance of the vessel only, which is categorized as "desire to receive" of any entity. For certainly this desire did not exist within the essence (Light) before creation.

12) Communion - (מהי דבקות) Similitude of phase which spiritual entities are drawn together and attach one to another. Diversity of phase creates distance between them.

13) Similarity - (מהי השואה) If there is no recognizable distinction of grades among the four gradations of the desire to receive, this is considered as complete similarity.

14) Extension - (מהי התפשטות) Light which departs from the framework of Emanator and becomes a phase of the emanated being is referred to as an extension of the Light. In actuality, the upper Light is not affected by this extension. It may be compared to a lit candle lighting another where the first candle does not undergo any diminution, and only in reference to the emanated being is there a concept of extension.

15) Pure - (מהו זך) The first phase of the desire to receive is distinguished as purer than the three grades which follow it. (cf. Inner Light 13, page 56)

16) Time - (מהו זמן) A definitive summation of phases which evolve from each other and affect each other in the order of cause and effect as the concept of periods of time of days, months and years.

17) Darkness - (מהו חושך) The fourth phase of desire which does not receive any light due to the Restriction is considered to be the root of darkness.

18) Wisdom - (מהי חכמה) Essence of the Light which is the life force of the emanated being.

19) Vacuum - (מהו חלל) The fourth phase which became emptied of the Light. It is considered darkness in relation to the Light. In relation to the vessel it is considered vacuum. The fourth phase itself is not lacking as an emanated being due to the Restriction but rather is considered vacuum without light.

20) Before and after - (מהם טרם ואחר–כך) When discussing a relationship between cause and effect, the cause is expressed as before and the effect as after.

21) Unified force and unified action -
(מהם יחיד ומיוחד) Unified whole indicates the upper Light which shines and dominates over all varying grades, which are different from each other so as to

transform this multiplicity to a unified whole. Unified action indicates and points to the final state of the action, which means after the unified force has already restored and created a likeness to the phase of the unit-ed force.

22) Unity - (מהו יחוד) Two dissimilar phases whose structures have become similar are considered to have united as one.

23) Right and left - (מהם ימין ושמאל) A lower grade which sometimes ascends to a dimension equal with one higher than it when the upper or higher requires the lower for its own completion. In this case the lower is considered as left and the upper grade is right.

24) Form - (מהו יוצר) The term form relates to the bestowed of the Light to the worlds, for this comprises all of existence, exclusive of the substance of the vessel.

25) Vessel - (מהו כלי) The desire to receive of the emanated being is its vessel.

26) Above - (מהו למעלה) A likeness of phase of the lower to the upper is considered as ascending above.

27) Emanator - (מהו מאציל) Every cause is known as Emanator to the phase which emerges from a cause known as the effect. The name Emanator includes the drawing of the Light and also the vessel that receives the Light.

28) A soul cut from the Light - (מהי מחצבת הנשמה) The desire to receive inherent in souls is what separates them and hews them from the upper Light, for diversity of phase is what separates in the realm of spirituality. And the subject of a soul being hewn refers to a transition from the World of Emanation to the World of Creation. This will be examined in the proper place.

29) Below - (מהו מטה) That which is considered less in grade than its companion is considered below the companion.

30) Unified action - (מהו מיוחד) see # 21.

31) Kingdom of the Ein Sof - (מהי מלכות דא״ס) This is the phase of the desire to receive that inevitably exists there.

32) From above to below - (מהו מלמעלה למטה) From phase one to phase four. The fourth phase that was left without Light is considered below all degrees and stages, Where the desire to receive is weaker, it is to be considered higher than the phase where the desire to receive is stronger, until the first phase which is above all others, i.e. the second, third and fourth phases.

33) Fills - (מהו ממלא) There is no trace of any lack, and there is no possibility to add to its completeness.

34) Above, below - (מהו מעלה מטה) The higher spiritual phase is known as above and that of an inferior grade is below.

35) Place - (מהו מקום) The desire to receive of the emanated being is known as "the place" for the abundance of the Light within it.

36) Cube - (מהו מרובע) The degree that includes within itself all four phases of the desire to receive.

37) Triangle - (מהו משולש) This is the grade that has only the first three phases of the desire to receive.

38) Contact - (מהו נוגע) If the degree of difference of form from the origin is not so recognizable as to create a separation from the root, it is referred to as "contact", "touching". This is the same matter between one phase and another.

39) The Middle Point - (מהי נקודה אמצעית) The fourth phase of the Endless is so referred to because of its proximity and connection with the Light of the Endless.

40) End - (מהו סוף) The end or terminating point of every emanated being is established by the power of restraint of the fourth phase, The upper Light desists from illuminating due to the fact that the emanated being does not desire to receive.

41) Circle - (מהם עגול, עגולים) If there is no difference of above or below among the four phases of the desire to receive, this condition is known as the circle. (This might be compared to the physical dimension of a circle where there is no distinction of above or below in a circle.) The four phases are therefore considered four circles, one within the other where it is impossible to distinguish the degree of above and below within them.

42) Upper - (מהו עליון) More spiritual.

43) Separation - (מהו פירוד) Two states of consciousness which are totally unlike each other are considered completely separated from each other.

44) Lack or open - (מהו פנוי) A place that is prepared to accept improvements and perfection.

45) Simple - (מהו פשוט) Where there is no distinction in consciousness or grades.

46) Contraction or Restriction - (מהו צמצום) Control over one's desires places Restriction on receiving despite a strong desire to receive This referred to as restricting oneself.

47) Line - (מהו קו) A concept that implies "above" and "below" which did not exist within the Endless. This idea also points to the existence of a diminished Light relative to the previous state.

48) Close - (מהו קרוב) Any consciousness phase which deems itself similar to its adjacent phase is considered to be nearer to it.

49) Head - (מהו ראש) That section or phase of the emanated being which has a greater similarity to the form of the root is called head.

50) Spirit - (מהו רוח) Light of Mercy is called spirit.

51) Desire - (מהו רצון פשוט) See #45

52) Name - (מהו שם) Holy or Metaphysical names are classifications as to how the Light which is hinted by these classifications comes to be grasped by our conscious minds; for example, that the name of a phase clarifies the path to understanding that phase.

53) Interior - (מהו תוך) When being received in its interior, the Light is considered as dwelling and limited within the vessel. When the Light is considered as being received outside the vessel, it then does not create any limitation on the Light that is received.

54) Motion - (מהי תנועה) Any new phase is considered movement in the spiritual or metaphysical realm due to its preparation from a prior phase of consciousness, and has emerged as a new consciousness, similar to physical separation of one section from another which moves out of its previous domain.

55) WHICH OF THE CONCEPTS IN KABBALAH CANNOT BE UNDERSTOOD WITH OUR SENSORY PERCEPTION?

Not even a single word in this wisdom, from beginning to end, can be understood by our sense or imagination within the frame of reference of space, time and motion and the like. Disappearance does not exist within the spiritual realm. Change of consciousness does not mean that there exists a disappearance from the first phase, but rather the first phase of consciousness remains as before without any change whatsoever. Whatever change does take place is considered an additional phase over and above the previous phase. (This might be compared to a lantern that is covered with several cloths. With each layer the light of the lantern becomes dimmer. However, the light of the lantern actually remains the same.)

56) WHAT IS THE USUAL LANGUAGE IN THE WISDOM OF KABBALAH?

This language is the "language of branches", which point to the upper roots, for there is not even a blade of grass below that does not have an upper energy motivation force. Therefore, the sages of Kabbalah found a language suitable to hint at within the branches and thus provide an understanding as to origin and cause.

57) What is that which fragments and causes separation in the metaphysical, spiritual realm of consciousness?

Diversity of consciousness or form separates and distances spiritual essence from one another.

58) What is the origin of the "desire to receive"?

The desire to share of the upper Light establishes the desire to receive in the emanated being.

59) How does the Lightforce exit from the realm of Emanator to become an emanated being?

Because of the form of consciousness of the desire to receive which newly emerged with the upper Light when It (the Light) desired to share, the new part went out or departed from the phase of Emanator and Cause, to become the phase of emanated being.

60) What is the first essence or substance of every emanated being?

The form that emerged anew and came into existence within the frame of "something from nothing" which is the "desire to receive", and is found in every existence, is considered the "first substance" to every emanated being and every existence. Furthermore, that which is something other than this substance is considered within the phase, degree, or frame of the Light. Bestowal which is drawn from the upper Light within the concept of "something from something", is not to be considered as included within the frame, concept, or consciousness of emanated or created being.

One may question how form becomes substance, or how one consciousness evolves from another. This is to be found in corporeality too, which is our nature when we wish to establish the first form of something, our attention can only be directed towards that which our senses can perceive. [That is, a wooden table can be seen as coming from a tree, and a tree from a seed. However, the internal, metaphysical realm of the seed cannot be grasped except by our own analysis of what emerged from the original, which in Kabbalah is referred to as the branches. We then *assume* that that which is observed on the physical scene undoubtedly also exists on the metaphysical level. For if not, how did the branches emerge?]

61) WHEN IS AN EMANATED BEING CONSIDERED SO?

Immediately at the first evolvement of the desire

to receive, which is called phase one of the desire, it is already considered as having gone out of the realm of emanator to that of the emanated.

62) A SPIRITUAL ENTITY THAT HAS RECEIVED WITHIN ITSELF A DIFFERENT PHASE, AND THEREFORE HAS BECOME SEPARATED FROM THAT PART AND IS CONSIDERED ANOTHER PHASE, DOES THE SPIRITUAL ENTITY UNDERGO ANY LOSS BECAUSE OF IT?

Disappearance or loss are terms that do not apply in spiritual essence. No segment that became isolated due to a change of form affects *any* loss or depreciation within the upper Light. This is compared to the lighting of one candle with another. The first candle is not affected by loss. Therefore any change of form or extension is to be considered as an addition to the previous state.

63) HOW AND NEAR WHOM ARE DISTINGUISHED OCCUR THE MULTITUDE SORTS OF FORMS (CONSCIOUSNESS) AND DIFFERENTIATIONS OF ALL THE WORLDS?

All of the additions and changes occur only within the effects and recipiency of the vessel from the Light. The Light, however, as respects to Itself always is found in a state of absolute rest without any trace of change or something new, whatsoever.

64) How do we formulate new events or motion within the Light?

There is no motion or new event within the Upper Light, only that entity which becomes emanated from the Upper Light. This is what is termed "new and varied according to the new forms of the vessel". For every entity recurs from the Light according to it's measurement of the desire to receive contained within it. Their phases and degrees are different one from another, and evolve one from another unlimited and never ending.

65) How could so many entities, at times in opposition to each other, that were drawn from It into the worlds, be included within this simple, quantified unity of the Light?

cf., Inner Reflection, 18, 29.

66) Through whom and what is the line drawn from the Endless?

The curtain, which means the power of prevention, takes place on the fourth phase after Tzimtzum (restriction) not accepting the Light within her vessel. This is responsible for the line to emerge from the Endless. The upper Light does not undergo any change through this process and shines (energizes) after the Tzimtzum as well as before Tzimtzum. It is only by virtue of the curtain that the vessel did not receive from the upper Light. Only within the first three phases was the Light permitted within the vessel since their measurement of desire to receive was weak relative to the receiving capacity of the fourth phase. And therefore the vessel received a thin line of Light relative to the capacity of the Light (Endless).

67) FOLLOWING THE TZIMTZUM, DID ANY CHANGES OCCUR WITHIN THE ENDLESS?

Although the fourth phase of the Endless restricted itself, nevertheless there is *no* occurrence of undressing or enclothing entities following the disappearance of the first entity as observed within the physical, corporeal world. Rather, here in the Endless, the nature of events is such that phases are additions over the prior phases where the prior phases do not move whatsoever, because there is no incidence of disappearance in spiritual essence.

Therefore the newly revealed incident of the departure of the Light, and the power of blocking that exists within the fourth phase not to receive within itself is to be considered as another new world unique to itself which is now added to the Light which (Light) remains as before without any change whatsoever. This is the understanding to be applied when observing any changes in the metaphysical, spiritual realm.

68) WHEN DID THE DENSENESS (INTENSITY) OF THE FOURTH PHASE BEGIN?

With the coming of the Line from the Endless on which the curtain placed its prevention on the Light to illuminate the fourth phase, only then did the denseness (intensity of the desire to receive in the fourth phase) become recognizable, for she was left without Light.

69) WHAT ARE THESE FOUR PHASES OF THE DESIRE TO RECEIVE?

At the outset the *Light* spreads and departs from the Emanator within the phase of Light of Wisdom which is the all inclusive Life force which belongs to the emanated being. And this is the first phase of the emanated being, and is also referred to as the first extension. Afterwards there is an arousal in this light phase which is a desire to impart (due to the containment of the Light by the emanated being). This arousal of the desire draws Light of Mercy from the Emanator. This is called the first arousal or phase two. Afterwards, the Light of Mercy is extended enormously with only a ray of Light of Wisdom and this is called the second extension or phase three (due to the emanated beings desire for Light of Mercy and not Light of Wisdom.) Afterwards, there is a return of an arousal for the all inclusive Light force which was the case in phase one. And with this arousal, the desire to receive was completed in ultimate growth and completeness, and this is called the second arousal or the fourth phase.

70) WHAT IS THE SIGNIFICANCE OF THE FOUR LETTERS OF THE TETRAGRAMMATON?

The *Yud* of the Tetragrammaton is the phase of the first extension of the Light which is called phase one. The first *Hei* of the Tetragrammaton which is the first arousal of the Light is called phase two. The *Vav* of the Tetragrammaton is the second extension of the Light which is called phase three. The final *Hei* of the Tetragrammaton is the second arousal of the Light and is called the fourth phase.

71) WHAT IS THE UPPERMOST HEAD OR TOP OF THE LINE WHICH TOUCHES THE ENDLESS?

cf., Inner Light 49.

72) WHAT IS THE UNIQUE, UNIFYING THOUGHT WHICH INCLUDES INFINITE

FORMS AND CONSCIOUSNESS, EVEN OPPOS-
ING ENTITIES OF EVERY AND ALL EXIS-
TENCE?

This is the thought to "bestow pleasure to his creatures."

73) AT WHICH POINT DO THE KABBALISTS BEGIN THEIR INQUIRY?

The subject matter discussed in the Wisdom of Kabbalah deals solely with the extension of the Light. However, as to that which pertains to the essence of the Light, there simply is no comprehension whatsoever.

74) WHAT ARE THE TWO PRINCIPLES THAT INCLUDE EVERYTHING?

The first principle is that whatever existence appears or will appear before us is already included and established in the Endless in all its features and final completeness. This phase is called the Endless [This might be compared to a seed that is all-inclusive of any future manifestations, ed.]. The second principle is that there are five subsequent worlds which are called: Primordial Man, Emanation, Creation, Formation and Action which evolve from the Malkhut (Kingdom) of the Endless after Restriction. And all that exists in the second principle emerges from the first principle.

75) What is the meaning of the phrase "He and his Name is One"?

The word "He" refers to the Light of the Endless. The word "His Name" points to the "desire to receive" of the Endless which is also noted as the Malkhut (Kingdom) of the Endless. "One" indicates that there does not exist any difference or change between the Light which is the secret of "He" and the vessel which is the secret of "His Name", and every entity (including the vessel) is Light.

76) What does the name "Endless" mean?

The state of existence before the Tzimtzum is called Endless to indicate that in that frame of reference there is no possibility of "end" whatsoever, inasmuch as even the fourth phase receives Light. Therefore, there is no cause there for an interruption of the Light resulting in an end.

77) What is drawn from the Desire to Receive that is included within the Endless?

Creation of the Worlds and all that is filled within them. It is for this reason that It restricted Itself within the fourth phase so as to reveal these worlds even unto this world of our existence. For in the world there is the possibility to convert and transform the consciousness for receiving to that of bestowing.

78) WHAT WAS THE REASON AND CAUSE FOR THE RESTRICTION OF THE LIGHT?

The idea of enhancement or elevation that the Malkhut (Kingdom) of the Endless saw as a stepping stone to an affinity with the form (consciousness) that formed her (Malkhut), which (enhancement) was only possible through the creation of the worlds due to restricting herself here (Malkhut).

79) WHICH PHASE OF RECEIVING CAN BE CONSIDERED A PHASE OF BESTOWAL?

When one receives *only* for the purpose of a consciousness to bestow.

80) TOWARDS WHAT END AND PURPOSE WAS THE TZIMTZUM PRODUCED?

So as to convert and transform the form and consciousness of receiving to a form of bestowal.

81) WHY DID THE LIGHT WITHDRAW FROM THE MIDDLE POINT AND NOT RETURN?

cf., Inner Light, 13, Inner Reflection, 22.

82) WHY DIDN'T THE PHASE OF "END" TAKE PLACE THROUGH THE TZIMTZUM?

Because the Tzimtzum did not occur as a result of a difference in form or consciousness that may have appeared or occurred in the desire to receive due to any lack that needed correction. The Tzimtzum took place not out of necessity due to a lack, rather only to elevate to a phase of enhancement.

83) WHY DID THE LIGHT WITHDRAW FROM ALL FOUR PHASES INSTEAD OF ONLY FROM THE PHASE OF MALKHUT WHERE THE ACTUAL TZIMTZUM TOOK PLACE?

Because there is no concept or consciousness of partiality in spirituality or metaphysics.

84) WHY DIDN'T A DIFFERENCE OF FORM OR CONSCIOUSNESS BE RECOGNIZ-ABLE - NAMELY, BETWEEN THE FOUR PHASES THERE WAS AN OBVIOUS DEGREE OF GRADATION, ONE LOWER THAN THE OTHER - AT THE TIME OF TZIMTZUM AND BEFORE THE COMING OR ADVENT OF THE LINE?

Before the appearance of the line, the fourth phase was not distinguishable as a denser and lower phase. And consequently, an impression of gradation because of her restriction did not occur.

85) How come the fourth phase did not become denser, less affinity with the Light immediately at the time and with the restriction of the Light, rather all four phases remained as one unified whole?

Because the Tzimtzum did not occur as a result of any difference in form or consciousness.

86) Which phase remained empty of the Light.

Only the fourth phase.

87) When shall the fourth phase again become filled with the Light?

When the vessel of receiving shall acquire a form of bestowal.

88) What caused the creation of the worlds?

The desire to receive which inevitably there (in the Endless) had a desire to enhance and elevate to the form and consciousness of the Light completely, and this was the cause for creation of the worlds.

89) WHAT IS THE ULTIMATE PURPOSE OF TORAH AND GOOD DEEDS?

To convert the vessel of receiving to one of a desire to bestow.

90) WHAT IS THE SEGULAH (THE OBJECTIVE FOR REWARD) OF THE REVELATION OF THE HOLY NAMES?

It is spiritually to convert the consciousness, or form of receiving, to one of bestowing.

91) HOW ARE THE HOLY NAMES REVEALED?

Through the efforts involved in Torah and good deeds.

92) WHAT IS MEANT BY THE END OF THE CORRECTION PERIOD?

When the vessel of receiving shall convert to one of bestowal.

93) WHAT IS THE SOURCE AND ORIGIN OF ALL CHAOS?

The difference in form and consciousness which exists between the "desire to receive" and the Emanator.

94) WHY IS IT IMPOSSIBLE TO CONVERT AND TRANSFORM THE VESSEL OF RECEIVING TO ONE OF BESTOWAL ONLY IN THIS MUNDANE WORLD AND NOT IN ANY OF THE OTHER UNIVERSES?

Because chaos and correction in one frame of reference can only exist in our mundane world.

95) WHAT ARE THE TWO PHASES OF LIGHT?

Light of Wisdom and Light of Mercy.

96) WHAT IS INCLUDED WITHIN THE EXTENSION OF THE LIGHT FROM THE EMANATOR?

The desire to bestow and the desire to receive.

97) WHICH LIGHT IS REVEALED WITH THE AROUSAL OF THE "DESIRE TO BESTOW"?

The Light of Mercy.

98) WHAT ARE THE TWO LIGHTS THAT ARE INCLUDED IN EVERY EMANATED BEING?

Light of Wisdom and Light of Mercy.

99) WHY IS THE LIGHT MERCY INFERIOR TO THE LIGHT OF WISDOM?

Because it is drawn to the emanated being by a desire and arousal originating within the emanated being.

100) WHEN DOES THE VESSEL OF RECEIVING BECOME A FINISHED, COMPLETE VESSEL AND CONSCIOUSNESS?

After the fourth phase of vessel or consciousness is revealed.

101) WHAT IS THE DIFFERENCE BETWEEN A VESSEL RECEIVING WITHIN ITS INTERIOR OR RECEIVING BY VIRTUE OF ITS EXTERIOR FORM OR CONSCIOUSNESS?

When the vessel receives into its interior, the vessel places a *limitation* according to its measurement and framework of its desire to receive upon the Light that it envelops and reveals, whereas when the vessels exterior consciousness occurs outside of itself, the vessel receiving at this stage does not place any limitation on the Light that it contains.

102) WHAT IS MEANT BY ENCIRCLING SFIROT?

When there does not exist a difference between above and below between the four levels of consciousness of the emanated being, there four levels are referred to as four circles, one within each other as the layers of an onion.

**103) WHY DOES THERE EXIST A DIFFEREN-
TIATION OF GRADES WITHIN THE CIRCLES,
ONE LOWER THAN THE OTHER BEFORE THE
COMING OF THE LINE?**

Since at the time of the Restriction (Tzimtzum) there was no feeling or consciousness of lack or inferiority due to the revealment of a change in dimensions of vessel and Light.

**104) IS THERE ANY NEGATIVITY OR CHAOS
THAT CAN BE ATTRIBUTED TO THE ESSENCE
OF ITS (DESIRE TO RECEIVE) CREATION?**

There is no inferiority in the essence of her creation. And with the Tzimtzum, there was no revealment of any deficiency other than the desire to receive became subject to restriction.

**105) WHAT IS THE MEANING OF THE
EXPRESSION "TO BE DRAWN INDIRECT
FROM THE EMANATOR"?**

cf., Inner Reflection, 19.

Rabbi Isaac Luria

A Biographical Sketch

(Excerpted from *Kabbalah for the Layman, Volume I,*
by Rabbi Philip S. Berg)

Rabbi Isaac Luria, the Ari haKadosh ("Holy Lion"), was born in Jerusalem in 1534. According to legend the Prophet Elijah appeared at his circumcision ceremony to act as Sandak (godfather), and told his father to take great care of the child, for he would be the source of an exalted light. After the death of his father, his mother, who was of Sephardic descent, took him to the home of her brother Mordekhai Francis, a wealthy and respected man in the Jewish community of Cairo. In Egypt, he studied with the famous Rabbis Betzalel and David Zimra (the Radbaz). At the age of seventeen he married one of his cousins.

The Ari was a Talmudic authority before he had reached the age of twenty, and soon mastered all the material his mentors had to offer him. He then discovered the Zohar, and lived as a hermit in a remote place by the Nile for thirteen years while he studied the secrets of the Kabbalah. In 1569 he settled in Safed, where he studied with Moses Cordovero and a circle of devoted disciples until he became a master in his own right.

Rabbi Moses Cordovero was drawn "as by a thirst" to the wisdom of Kabbalah in 1522; he studied in Safed with Rabbi Solomon Alkabetz, whose sister he married. He proved a gifted teacher and writer, composing the first comprehensive commentary on the Zohar (Or Yakar, the Exalted Light). The manuscript, obtained on microfilm from the Vatican Library, has already yielded many volumes of priceless teachings. His other major works include Or Ne'erav, Shiur Komah, Tomer Deborah, and Pardes Rimonim.

The Ari developed a new system for understanding the mysteries of the Zohar: called the Lurianic method, it focuses on the Ten Sfirot or Luminous Emanations, and sheds new light on the hidden wisdom of the Kabbalah. His complete understanding of the mysteries of the Zohar, together with the other great powers that he manifested during his lifetime, were a result of his unique spiritual identity. His student, aim Vital, tells the following story:

One day I went with my teacher [the Ari] to the site where Rabbi Shimon and his disciples had assembled and created the Greater Assembly. On the eastern side of the path was a stone containing two large fissures; the northern fissure was where Rabbi Shimon had sat, and the southern one where Rabbi Abba had sat. At a nearby tree, facing these two clefts, Rabbi Elazar had been seated. The Ari seated himself within the northern fissure, as Rabbi Shimon had done before him, and I sat within the southern one, not knowing that this was the seat of Rabbi Abba. It was only after this encounter that my teacher explained to me the significance of what had taken place. Now I know what he had in mind when he told me that I contain the spark of one of the members of the Idra (assembly).

Anyone familiar with the writings of the Ari will realize that his clarity and depth of thought and understanding could only come from one blessed with the spirit of Rabbi Shimon. Only Rabbi Shimon's soul would have been capable of the feats of transcendence that are clearly indicated in the Ari's writings. Some people thought that the Ari was the harbinger of the Messianic Age, and an extraordinary legend grew up concerning his piety and righteousness. One Erev Shabbat (Sabbath eve) the Ari assembled his disciples and declared that he could effect the coming of the Messiah that very Shabbat. He stressed to all present the importance of complete harmony, warning them to be aware of the slightest confrontation with one another. So the unique Shabbat began, and all went well throughout Friday night and Shabbat morning. Towards the close of Shabbat, a trivial argument broke out among the children of the Ari's disciples. This quarrel escalated until the parents intervened, leading in turn to a disagreement among two of the disciples. Shabbat ended without the appearance of the Messiah;

the disciples showed their disappointment at being unworthy of his coming, and asked their teacher the reason for this. The Ari replied sadly, "For a small pittance the arrival of the Messiah was forestalled." Little did his disciples know that Satan resorts to any means to divert men from their noble intentions. Knowing all too well the disciples' awareness of the important task of maintaining harmony among themselves, he chose a covert and unsuspected approach to gain his objective of disunity. "Thus," concluded the Ari, "the coming of the Messiah does not mean that we must wait for some individual to ride through the gate of Mercy in the Eastern Wall of the city of Jerusalem, mounted on a white donkey. Rather, the presence of goodwill towards men and peace on earth, as indicated in the verse 'The wolf shall dwell with the lamb, and the leopard shall lie down with the kid' (Isaiah 11:6), is the Messiah. The Messiah is nothing more than the symbol of world harmony". Hearing this, the disciples departed with bowed heads.

On another occasion the Ari gathered his disciples together for a journey to Jerusalem in order to spend Shabbat there. When they heard his intention they were overcome with bewilderment and asked their teacher how he could contemplate such a long journey when the arrival of the Shabbat was only a matter of minutes away. Smiling, the Ari replied, "The elements of time, space and motion are merely an expression of the limitations imposed by the physical body on the soul. When the soul has sway over the body, however, these limiting factors cease to exist. Let us now proceed to Jerusalem, therefore, for our corporeal bodies have lost their influence over our souls". In this way, singing mystical chants, the Ari and his disciples arrived in Jerusalem in time to celebrate the coming of the Sabbath.

At the age of thirty-eight, on the fifth day of Av 1572, the Ari completed his task on earth and ascended to the place waiting for him in the Garden of Eden.

To his most trusted and favored pupil aim Vital, and to aims son, Shmuel Vital, the Ari gave the task of recording his thoughts and teachings on paper as a record for posterity for the Golden Age of Kabbalah in Safed. These two devoted followers summarized, as far as was possible, the deeds and wisdom of their teacher, producing the volumes that we now regard as the Ari's writings. aim Vital became a legendary figure and a source of wisdom for later Kabbalists, who could now refer to a concise and clear literary work that laid open the heretofore obscure and abstruse contents of the central work of Kabbalistic literature, the Zohar.

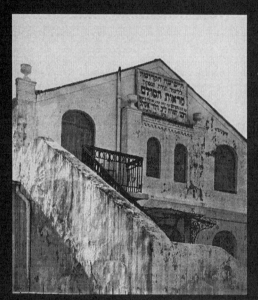

The first Kabbalah Learning Centre (Yeshivat Kol Yehuda), circa 1925, founded by the great Kabbalist, Rabbi Yehuda Ashlag.

The tomb of Rabbi Ashlag, (1886-1955) the most influential Kabbalist in the 20th Century. Har Ha'menuchot, Jerusalem, Israel.

A Biographical Sketch

(Excerpted from *Kabbalah for the Layman, Volume I*,
by Rabbi Philip S. Berg)

I was told of Rabbi Ashlag's life and personality by my Master Rabbi Yehudah Z. Brandwein, who was his disciple. Rabbi Ashlag was born in Warsaw in 1886 and was educated in Hasidic schools. In his early years, he was a student of Rabbi Shalom Rabinowitz of Kalushin and of his son Yehoshua Asher of Porissor. He emigrated to Palestine in 1919 and settled in the Old City of Jerusalem. Rabbi Brandwein spoke of him as a man with immense powers of meditation, a man to whom the world of metaphysics and mysticism were as familiar as was the world of physics to Einstein. The comparison is not altogether without significance, since it was during Rabbi Ashlag's lifetime that great advances and discoveries were being made in the world of science, destroying many of the traditional scientific theories of stability, permanence and purpose in the universe. The great monument of that scientific era, Einstein's Theory of Relativity, confirmed what Kabbalists had known to be true for centuries — that time, space and motion are not immutable constants but a function of energy. Rabbi Ashlag pioneered a new system for understanding the works of the Ari. In his sixteen-volume textbook, the Study of the Ten Luminous Emanations (Talmud Eser haSfirot) he devised a logical system through which the essence of the transcendent realm was transmitted by means of an array of symbols and illustrations. These, he felt, best described those aspects of the teachings of the Ari that were beyond the grasp of the intellect alone. The Ten Luminous Emanations deals with those concepts that have eluded the most determined scholars for centuries. The intimate relationship between the physical and metaphysical realms is presented simply, together with a description of the series of evolution's that culminate in the world we know today, and also a detailed presentation of those motives that may be ascribed to the Creator.

The restoration of a mystical approach in the world of Kabbalah, as opposed to the dry study of ritual and ceremony for its own sake, draws a large part of its strength from the link between the concepts expressed by the author and his mystical consciousness.

In addition to these volumes, Rabbi Ashlag's monumental work on the Zohar has had a great influence on Judaic studies and marks a turning point in the attempt to render the Kabbalah comprehensible to contemporary students. His was the first translation of the entire Zohar into modern Hebrew. Realizing that a comprehensive translation would not be sufficient on its own, he also composed a commentary on the most difficult passages, and compiled a volume of diagrams describing the process of the evolution of the Sfirot in all their manifestations down to the level of this world.

Generally speaking, Kabbalists of the rank and stature of Rabbi Ashlag receive their knowledge through Divine revelation. They tend to be men with a broad rabbinic education, and Rabbi Ashlag was no exception in this respect. More penetrating, however, was his knowledge of the spectrum of Kabbalah, and his translation of the Zohar shows clearly that he was knowledgeable in every known science.

NOTES